REMEMBER THE ALAMO BOWL

Bram Kohlhausen's Epic TCU Comeback

By Jim Reeves

Hope is the thing with feathers
That perches in the soul,
And sings the tune without the words,
And never stops at all.
Emily Dickinson

BERKELEY PLACE BOOKS

Remember the Alamo Bowl
Bram Kohlhausen and TCU's Epic Comeback
By Jim Reeves

To my dad, who always made time to play catch.

• • •

Editor: Amy Culbertson
Book designer: Tom Johanningmeier
Cover designer: Kari Lindner Crane
Cover photo: Courtesy of Texas Christian University

1st edition 10 9 8 7 6 5 4 3 2 1

Berkeley Place Books
An imprint of Great Texas Line Press
Post Office Box 11105
Fort Worth, Texas 76110
TEL 817-922-8929 / FAX 817-926-0420

Printed in USA by Hill Printing Solutions, Dallas, Texas

Contents

Prologue: *The Lowest Point* 4

Chapter 1: *Starting Young* 16

Chapter 2: *'El Capitan'* 23

Chapter 3: *'Houston, We Have a Problem'* 30

Chapter 4: *A California Reality Check* 38

Chapter 5: *Seeing Purple* 43

Chapter 6: *A Devastating Blow* 52

Chapter 7: *Party on the River Walk* 62

Chapter 8: *Catastrophe at the 11th Hour* 70

Chapter 9: *Game Day* 83

Chapter 10: *Halftime Blues* 94

Chapter 11: *Purple Rain* 102

Chapter 12: *Overtime* 121

Chapter 13: *Full Circle* 130

Epilogue: *An Unlikely Hero* 135

Where They Are Now 141

About the Author 144

Prologue

The Lowest Point

EVEN IN A STATE of shock, Bram Kohlhausen knew the drill. Whatever the score, whatever the circumstance, at halftime of every football game TCU's players routinely gather on the field around head coach Gary Patterson before heading into the locker room.

This time, though, whatever the coach had to say to his team in those few moments on the evening of Jan. 2, 2016, halfway through the Alamo Bowl in San Antonio, Texas, Bram was too stunned to listen. He lingered numbly on the fringe of the scrum of almost 120 players. He didn't really need to hear whatever Patterson might be saying — the Alamodome scoreboard screamed the story loud and clear.

No. 15 Oregon 31, No. 11 TCU 0.

As he slowly joined his teammates at the rim of the circle around Patterson, it was all Bram could do to keep from weeping. Or gagging. The same could have been said of many a TCU fan, given how badly the Frogs were doing against the Ducks on this cold, rainy afternoon in south-central Texas. Oregon weather, the fans grumbled to each other, even though they were dry and warm inside the jam-packed indoor bedlam of the temperature-controlled Alamodome. It was the embattled Horned Frogs who were feeling the heat.

The die-hard TCU fans knew the shockingly lopsided score at the end of the first half wasn't the reason for TCU's on-field huddle. It was simply Patterson's standard operating procedure: He always wanted his players' immediate attention and focus. He wanted them under some semblance of control and together as a team at halftime before exiting the field as one.

Certainly, one thing his players needed at that moment was simple routine, a reminder of how things were supposed to be in what had been one of college football's most successful programs since Patterson's arrival in Fort Worth in December 2000. By the time the Frogs were ready to head for the tunnel after their brief muster, the last of the Oregon players had already filed into the visitors' locker room, ready to celebrate their glorious first half and to get a jump on their post-game celebrations.

Not eager to come eye-to-eye with Patterson after the first-half debacle, Bram Kohlhausen had lingered at the periphery of the TCU players. The sounds of the screaming fans and the grumbling of his disheartened teammates swirled around him along with whatever unhappy message his head coach was conveying. But the only thing on Bram's mind at that moment was the dawning realization that his college career was over. He'd had one last shot and blown it, just as he had so many other chances. There was no way around it.

In his only major college start, in his senior year, when his team had needed him the most, Bram believed he had failed miserably — far worse than he could have ever imagined. He was certain, without a shred of doubt, that he was headed to an ignominious seat on the end of the bench in the second half while some other TCU quarterback tried in vain to dig the Frogs out of this impossible 31-point abyss. If Bram could have slit open a seam in the Alamodome's artificial grass, he would have gratefully crawled beneath the carpet and made it his final resting place, never to be seen again.

But Bram had to follow his teammates into the TCU locker room and face the music — a funeral dirge for his college football career, he felt sure. He had to confront his peers, his friends, his teammates. He had to meet with offensive coordinators Sonny Cumbie and Doug Meacham, two men who had believed in him when no one else did. That would be especially painful.

It was Meacham who had been most responsible for Bram Kohlhausen's winding up at TCU in the first place. But whatever trust, whatever loyalty Meacham may have felt for him had surely been destroyed in the span of the last 30 horrific minutes. How could Bram look Meacham in the eye now?

Then there was Patterson, the indomitable and fiery head coach who had pulled him aside before the team bus left the hotel to deliver an emotional message that had put an even bigger lump in Bram's throat than was already there.

"Hey, man, you're going to be the starter," Bram would recall the coach saying. "Go out there and play for your dad. I have faith in you, and if anyone's going to help you out, it'll be your dad upstairs."

These had been haunting words for the young man who was about to start his first TCU game as quarterback, for Bram Kohlhausen had lost his father to cancer just two months earlier. At the moment they were uttered, they had seemed like a whispered prayer, a foundation for Bram's resolve. Now he wasn't sure that even divine intervention could bail the Frogs out of this bottomless pit.

He could only imagine how disappointed and disheartened Bill Kohlhausen would have been if he had been in the stands. Conflicting emotions roiled in Bram's heart: gratitude that Bill wasn't there to see his youngest son humiliated in front of the world; despair that his father never would be there again.

Bill Kohlhausen had died Nov. 7, at his home in Houston, two painful years after receiving his initial diagnosis. The man who had most believed in Bram's ability to play football hadn't lived to see his son make a single major college start.

Bram had been with the Horned Frogs in Stillwater, Okla., when he learned of his father's passing early on the morning of TCU's game with Oklahoma State. Even though he knew it was imminent, his dad's death had shaken Bram's world as nothing ever had before.

• • •

It had been Bill Kohlhausen's dream to see Bram as the starting quarterback in a major college bowl game. Up until two days before this final game of his senior year, though, Bram had already given up on that dream.

Bram had been a walk-on at TCU in the fall of 2014, so far down on the depth chart at that point that a scholarship wasn't on the table. He had worked his way into a backup role as a junior behind Trevone Boykin, who was on his way to becoming one of the best quarterbacks in TCU history and a Heisman Trophy candidate. The two had quickly become best friends and roommates.

From the time he'd arrived at TCU, Bram had known that the only way he'd ever start a game would be if Boykin suffered an injury. Maybe not even then. The coaches might decide to go with one of the younger quarterbacks, as they had when Boykin was nursing an injury a few weeks earlier: They'd picked redshirt freshman Foster Sawyer to start against Oklahoma, even though Bram was technically No. 2 on the depth chart.

That one had turned out OK for Bram, though: Sawyer had struggled, and Bram had led the Frogs on a comeback that fell just short of an upset of the Sooners.

But the flamboyant and multi-talented Boykin was TCU's star attraction. With Boykin back at the helm, the Frogs and fans had been confident they could handle Oregon in the Alamo Bowl. Trevone was in the driver's seat, and Bram Kohlhausen was the near-forgotten wingman. His job: Sit back and enjoy the ride; the ebullient and popular Boykin would take them home victorious.

So both players and fans had been in a celebratory mood in San Antonio in the days leading up to the game on Saturday, and the cantinas along the city's festive River Walk were handy to help them do it. The mariachis played; the margaritas flowed.

Then, in the wee morning hours on Thursday, New Year's Eve, after assistant coaches had safely tucked their star quarterback into his room at the midnight curfew check, cellphones in the hotel rooms of TCU officials, coaches and players had begun buzzing. Boykin had been arrested after a 2 a.m. bar fight just a few doors down from the team hotel. He'd punched a policeman.

Among all the frantic calls and texts unleashed by Boykin's arrest that morning had been one from Coach Meacham to his No. 2 quarterback at 4 a.m.: Bram would be Boykin's replacement on Saturday. By late afternoon, Boykin had been bailed out of jail by a TCU official, suspended by Patterson and promptly dispatched back to Fort Worth, never to wear a TCU uniform again. In a little over 48 hours, the obscure wingman with the strange name, Bram Kohlhausen, would be making his first-ever start at quarterback in a major college football game.

As the Boykin news broke, the gasp of anguish from TCU fans echoed from the Alamo City to Cowtown and back again. Boykin *was* the TCU offense. It all revolved around him and his dynamic play-making. The impact was felt farther west, in the casino sports books of Las Vegas, where the betting line immediately went from TCU by 1 to Oregon by 7, a breathtaking eight-point swing overnight.

• • •

Walking in a daze toward the TCU locker room after the game's first half, Bram would have given anything if his team could have been only eight points behind the Ducks. Desperate for the chance to redeem himself, he briefly fantasized that Coach Patterson would be too concerned with a defense that had surrendered an almost inconceivable 31 points in two quarters to worry about him.

He figured his best chance of being allowed to start the second half would come if the decision were left to coaches Cumbie and Meacham. Still, he expected one of them to approach him shortly to notify him they'd decided to go with Sawyer in the second half.

Given the circumstances, the move seemed inevitable. Why keep playing the walk-on non-scholarship senior who had just led his team into a 31-0 ditch when a younger, highly recruited quarterback, one who would be returning next season, might possibly light a spark under the team, meanwhile gaining some valuable experience?

Bram understood that reasoning as well as anyone. It didn't mean he had to like it. How could he face his mom or his two big brothers? Or all the friends who had scrambled for tickets to the game at the last minute because they'd heard that Bram would be starting in place of Boykin? There were

64,569 fans in the sold-out stadium and 7.4 million more watching on TV, and his humiliation was being played out in front of all of them.

At the Alamo Bowl, the teams — usually in second or third place in their respective conferences — alternate each year between the home and visitors' locker rooms. Since this was the Big 12's year to be home team, TCU occupied the home locker room. The Oregon Ducks were assigned the visitors' quarters, Locker Room D, first on the left and closer to the field than the home-team quarters.

Bram had just reached that point in the Alamodome tunnel when he began hearing something other than the muted roar of his own thoughts. Inside their locker room, the Oregon Ducks were partying as if they were already swigging margaritas on the River Walk. Mortified, because he knew his teammates were hearing the same thing, Bram put his head down and kept walking, wondering if he would ever wake up from this insane nightmare.

Though some of today's memories of that evening in the Alamodome can be a bit blurry for Bram, he doesn't have any trouble recalling that moment.

"I could hear them whooping and hollering," he recalls. "They were saying things like, 'We got this! Keep rollin'! We can put up 62!'

"You just feel embarrassed, just walking by. You don't want to make eye contact with anyone in the tunnel or even in the locker room. You feel like a wounded dog with his tail between his legs."

Bram tried to follow his usual halftime routine: Hit the head; grab a Gatorade and some peanut-butter crackers to refuel. He walked out of the urinals just in time to see TCU linebacker coach Jason Phillips pick up a trash can and hurl it across the room.

"This isn't TCU football!" Bram remembers hearing Phillips scream. "You're embarrassing me and everyone who played before you guys!"

"I walked right past that and thought, 'Shit, this guy's serious. He might throw me across the room next.' One of the players — I think it might have been Garrett Kaufman [the Frogs linebacker who had blocked a first-half Oregon punt only to have the Ducks recover it for a first down] — slapped me on the shoulder and said, 'We got this. We got faith in you.' In my head, I'm thinking, 'Do you really? We're down 31-0. I'm not an idiot.' "

Bram's locker was the second on the left from the locker-room entrance. The first one, now jarringly empty, had belonged to Boykin. Bram ducked his head, walked straight to his locker and sat facing into it. He didn't want to talk to anyone, didn't want to look anyone in the eye. He pulled on his headphones. If he had music playing, he doesn't remember what it was now.

"When I got to my locker I was thinking, 'I'm gonna get pulled. I'm never playing football again. It's over.' I was just waiting for Coach Cumbie or another of the coaches to come up to me and just tell me, 'We're going to go with Foster this half.'

"I didn't really want to talk to the other quarterbacks," he recalls. "I just wanted to keep my nose down and have tunnel vision."

At halftime, TCU's quarterbacks always meet with the offensive coaches. Within minutes, an assistant coach walked over to Bram and the other quarterbacks. "Coach Cumbie wants to meet with you guys," he said. Crossing the locker room on the way to the coaches' dressing room, Bram looked up and saw Patterson coming the other way.

"I remember not wanting to make eye contact with him

at all, but he barely noticed me. He was pissed off at his defense more than he was the offense. He was on the way to talk to the defense."

Bram was happy to be headed in the opposite direction.

He crowded into the coaches' dressing room with Foster Sawyer and third-team freshman quarterback Grayson Muehlstein, joining offensive coordinators Cumbie and Meacham, running backs coach Curtis Luper, offensive line coach Jarrett Anderson and receivers coach Rusty Burns.

It was Cumbie and Meacham who did most of the talking, Anderson chiming in with suggestions on plays that might work in the second half. Cumbie, addressing Bram directly, broke down each first-half drive.

"He was like, 'Incomplete pass, gain of 5, first down, 15-yard penalty' . . . that seemed to be the trend. We'd get something going, get a first down, then we'd get an unsportsmanlike conduct [call] and back up 15 yards. Then we'd go three and out. Inconsistency was killing us. I remember Cumbie saying, 'We're doing everything correct, but we're getting stupid penalties and shooting ourselves in the foot.' "

The loudest thing in the room, however, was what wasn't being said. No one, so far, had told Bram that he was out of the game, that Sawyer would start the second half. Cumbie was talking to him as he would to any quarterback he fully expected to play in the second half.

"The one criticism he had was about the interception I threw. It was a horrible read, and he said we can't do that in the course of the game. He said, 'If we're going to come back in this game, we have to take care of the football.' It didn't take much football IQ to know what needed to happen. It was simple. We had to score every drive and not let them score at all. Not even once. But what were the chances?"

The ESPN telecast was already providing the answer to that question, at least to those of its viewers who hadn't already changed the channel. They were learning that, with a 31-0 lead and two quarters to play, Oregon mathematically had a 99.1 percent chance of winning the game.

As the quarterbacks were listening to the coaches, Bram looked up and saw Patterson walking back into the coaches' dressing room. The coach went to his locker and began stripping off his sweat-soaked black knit shirt. Before donning a new one, he turned to the three quarterbacks in the room.

"You know, guys, this isn't Frog football," Patterson rasped in his trademark hoarse bark. "We have to continue to fight."

Then he pulled on a fresh shirt — a purple one.

• • •

Bram Kohlhausen was more than willing to keep fighting; he just couldn't believe he was going to get the chance. He still doesn't remember whether anyone ever actually told him he would start the second half.

"Coach Cumbie might have told me they were going to let me finish the game, but I don't remember that specifically. He could have, though. That whole halftime, that whole game, was kind of like a blur. Everything was happening so quickly, it's hard to break it down. Essentially, I was in a state of shock.

"But nobody ever came up to me and told me I was out, so I put my helmet on and got ready to play."

The reality that he was going to be left in to start the second half at quarterback was beginning to sink in for Bram. Surprisingly, it didn't feel as good as he thought it would. In fact, the idea left him more than a little terrified. *What if the second half was a repeat of the first?*

In the stands, the TCU fans' spirits had hit rock bottom. Bram's brother Gareth was so discouraged he was asking other family members if they should just leave. It was too sickening to watch, too painful.

TCU's first-half collapse had been a disheartening development for those on the business end of the game, too. As was her halftime habit, the Alamo Bowl's vice president of operations, Julie Baker, headed from her usual spot at the sidelines to the tunnel for a quick break. The first person she ran into there was TCU's director of football operations, Matt Lewis.

"Matty Lew was apologizing profusely," Baker recalls, "because we both knew TV sets were switching channels or being turned off by the thousands across the country. Now, more often than not, our [Alamo Bowl] games go down to the wire for some reason. We've had tons of close games, so maybe it was that, or for whatever reason, I just told him, 'The game's not over yet.' "

• • •

Back at his locker, as the minutes ticked on toward what would be the final moments of Bram Kohlhausen's college-football career, Bram could hear Patterson and the assistant coaches still berating the defense, background noise to the thoughts streaming through his head.

"You start thinking, just let me stay in the locker room, don't make me go back out there. You just want to cower down and quit. But another part of me is saying, 'You've got to get up and go do it.'

"I've always been a competitor. I'd competed every single spring, every summer, every fall camp, to be a [college] starter, and I was just never good enough.

"I remember competing in the backyard, on the basketball court; I always wanted to win. At TCU, I never felt we were going to lose.

"But when you're down 31-0 against Oregon, you have

the realization that this time we're going to lose. I'm going to go home. I don't want to talk to the media, I don't want to talk to you guys [his teammates], because I let all of you down.

"Then there's that part of you that says, 'I'm going to go out there, and I'm going to kick some ass and everybody's going to come with me. And if you don't, we'll put somebody else in.' "

And now strength and conditioning coach Don Sommer was striding through the locker room, giving players the five-minute warning . . . three minutes . . . then it was, "Let's roll!"

"Coming out of the tunnel, I was like, this is really embarrassing for me. It's embarrassing for my friends who made the drive to San Antonio to watch the game. It's embarrassing for my family. I was thinking, 'We've at least got to make this respectable.'

"I didn't want to be that guy, going back to my neighborhood and hearing about how you got blown out by Oregon. I wanted to be that guy who won — or at least put up a fight."

Make it respectable, Bram told himself. Don't quit. Don't hide. Don't run from it. Meet it head on.

The Bram Kohlhausen who had come slinking through that tunnel 30 minutes earlier was not the resolute young quarterback who now trotted back through it and onto the Alamodome turf for the second half.

Bram Baker Kohlhausen was being given a second chance. Redemption, not just for the Frogs' terrible first half but for everything he had lost or frittered away over the last five years, was at hand.

Chapter 1
Starting Young

DONNA KOHLHAUSEN WAS an unabashed lover of literature, especially fiction: all genres, any author, any subject. She loved everything about reading — the way authors wove their plots and stories, the characters they created, the adventures that unfolded and took her to faraway places. It was natural, then, in the Houston summer of 1992, for a pregnant Donna Kohlhausen to settle on her third son's name the same way she'd chosen those of his two older brothers — from a book she was reading at the time.

During Donna's first pregnancy, she'd become engrossed with the mystery novel *The Maltese Falcon.* Dash, born in September of 1980, was named after author Dashiell Hammett, creator of hard-boiled detective Sam Spade.

Nine years later, young Dash was reading *King Arthur and the Knights of the Round Table* for a school assignment and left the book lying on the breakfast bar one day. Thumbing through it, the very pregnant Donna was intrigued by the name of Sir Gareth, younger brother of Sir Gawain. She mentioned the name that night in a phone conversation with her husband, on a golf junket in Ireland. Bill Kohlhausen told her he'd just seen a commentator on local TV named Gareth — and that his caddy that day had been named Gareth too. It seemed, Donna would say later, that it was in the stars for their second son to be christened Gareth.

No need to hire Hammett's iconic private eye Sam Spade, then, to figure out how the youngest of the Kohlhausen brood got his first name. Two years after Gareth arrived, Donna was deep into Bram Stoker's *Dracula* while pregnant with her third child. Obviously, Count Dracula wasn't a possibility as a name for a newborn baby. But Bram — that name was just different enough to be interesting. Plus, the alliteration with Baker, the family name that would be her third son's middle name, had a sweet ring to it. Bram Baker Kohlhausen was born Aug. 7, 1992.

Bram's oldest brother Dash, Donna would later recall, had displayed the overachieving drive of so many first sons. He was studious, well-behaved, a great student. He was a hard worker, never flustered; "the best kid in the whole world," she often told friends.

Dash was an athlete, too. Some of Bram's earliest memories would be of watching his oldest brother play first base for Houston's Lamar High, where Bram himself would later excel. An excellent left-handed hitter, Dash would go on to play college baseball at Trinity University in San Antonio, where he once held the school record for doubles in a season (19, in 2000).

Gareth was the most gregarious of the three brothers. He made friends easily and everywhere. He was fun-loving, smoothly melding into whatever group was at hand. If there was a party going on, Gareth would inevitably be at the riotous center of it. He could walk into a room and steal the show.

Gareth was smart, too, in a different way from Dash, who

Bram played football in middle school at St. Michael and started as a sophomore at Lamar in Houston.

would later be heading into the realm of corporate law. Gareth would become the family's Mr. Fixit, with a quick grasp of how almost anything mechanical worked. He installed ceiling fans, hung TVs. Anything electronic he could take apart and put back together again.

Gareth's larger-than-life personality was matched by his physical size — eventually reaching 6 feet tall and 250 pounds. With the family's natural athleticism, Gareth became a gifted offensive lineman in high school and spent a season playing football for Trinity U.

Bram, though . . . it seemed that Bram was born to be the quarterback. Almost as soon as he could walk, it seemed that he was running instead. Everywhere. And fast.

"Bram was always the fastest, the strongest; climbed the highest," Donna recalls. "He was just an incredible athlete from the time he was a tiny kid. He was totally different from the other two. As the youngest, he was always loved, never a day's trouble. He loved athletics, loved playing every sport. In baseball, he was a natural shortstop.

"His personality was quiet. When everyone else was being noisy — Bill was a little hard of hearing and often talk-

Courtesy of Donna Kohlhausen

The Kohlhausen boys in 1998, from left: Bram, his half-brother Trey and brothers Gareth and Dash.

ed loudly — Bram would whisper. One day when he was about 4, he came up to me and asked, 'Am I invisible?' I said, 'No, you're not invisible; why would you ask that?' And he said, 'Because whenever I call your name, you don't answer.' "

• • •

Donna Pendergast had been practicing general law and involved in a lot of trial work when she met Bill Kohlhausen. It was at a campaign rally on Nov. 9, 1977, and Bill, also a lawyer, was escorting a woman who was running for mayor of Houston. It was raining. Bill loaned Donna his umbrella. Two years later, they were married. It was a second go-round for Bill, who already had a grown son, Trey, from his first marriage.

Certainly, the three boys Donna and Bill would go on to welcome into their family inherited at least some of their athletic gifts from their father. A scratch golfer, Kohlhausen, known on the course as "Billy," was the city amateur champion of Houston on multiple occasions.

Bill, a personal-injury attorney, was "an ambulance chaser," Donna says fondly. Bram remembers that his dad had a network of taxi drivers, paramedics and even police officers who would tip him off on potential cases. It was a lucrative practice, especially before tort reform, and it helped provide a comfortable upper-middle-class living. The Kohlhausens never considered themselves wealthy, though: What they had they mostly poured into raising their sons.

"It was just a very supporting home," Bram recalls. "There was no drama. Both my parents worked, but they were at every game. I had grandparents who truly cared. There was never anything crazy about my childhood.

"If I needed something, I pretty much had it — a new bat, a new glove, whatever. I had a blessed childhood. We didn't travel a lot, because of sports, except to go skiing in the winter. We'd go to Breckenridge, Vail, Aspen, Telluride. We did go to Cabo (San Lucas) once and Cozumel. But we really didn't take annual family vacations" every summer.

"My memories of my brothers are almost all sports-related. My earliest memory is swimming in our backyard with them, or running around the neighborhood. We could walk across the street into Memorial Park and play catch. Just down the street was Memorial Park Golf Course, one of the best public courses in Houston. We'd walk down there with my dad most mornings in the summer and hit practice balls.

"We would go as a family to watch Dash's baseball games at Houston Lamar. My dad never missed a game."

Dash recalls spending a lot of time with his little brother when Bram was little:

"I guess my dad was 54 and my mom was 40 when they had Bram. He was the youngest, and he kind of had free rein. He learned to ride a bike without training wheels when he was 3. He was always running around with me and Gareth and our friends.

"I went off to college when he was around 6. He was just always in the middle of everything. He was always very athletic, always one of the better players on whatever team he was on. He constantly wanted to run places, never wanted to walk. Everything was always a race or a sprint."

Like Dash, Bram would excel at baseball. But when he turned 6, Bram told his parents he wanted to play football. An avid football fan himself, Bill was thrilled. He took Bram to watch a youth league football game, and they came home toting a full set of pads.

Because his birthday fell in August, it turned out that Bram could get a waiver to begin playing immediately. He was still younger than most of the boys, and initially the coach played him only for the minimum time required. But by the end of the season Bram was on the field the entire game.

His father couldn't have been more delighted.

"Bill adored football," Donna said. From then on until illness curtailed his traveling during Bram's college career, Bill Kohlhausen would never miss a game Bram played. He coached Bram's age-12 Gators football team to a league championship; he coached his son's age-10 and -12 baseball teams too.

Where once it was Dash, then Gareth, whose games brought the family together, now it was Bram. Everyone in the family believed that the youngest son was an athletic prodigy. He had a chance to be something special.

"Bram was just fun to be around," Gareth recalls. "I remember him canceling play dates and not going to other kids' birthday parties so that he could play ball with me and my friends," holding his own with boys two years his elder.

"He was way more athletic than I was. He was the little

brother, though, so I would make him let me win. He was just a nice kid, kind of quiet, really. He worked hard, and he loved baseball and football."

Indeed, Bram played baseball, football and basketball through middle school and starred in all three. His size and natural athletic ability made him a force in youth basketball, where he once scored 30 points in a church-league championship game.

When he'd arrived at St. Michael Catholic School ready to play middle-school football, Bram found that the coach's son was already installed as the starting quarterback. Not for long. Once the coach got a good long look at Bram — his arm strength, his speed, his natural leadership — the coach's son found himself at running back and Bram comfortably settled into his accustomed position behind center.

Meanwhile, he was learning some lessons about sports that went beyond sheer athleticism.

"When I came home from law school, Bram was 14," Dash recalls. "I started coaching the 13-14-year-old division in our old Little League. In that league, dads couldn't coach their kids. I had to really work hard to draft him and had to trade a bunch of draft picks away to be able to get him. I wound up with Bram and one other 14-year-old kid. The rest were 13-year-olds.

"Bram was pissed off when he saw the team around him. He said, 'Dash, I don't know these kids.' He wasn't happy, but it turned out to be a good experience for him. It taught him to be a leader.

"The other kids weren't on the same level he was as a player, but over the course of the year he really learned a lot about how to lead, to put his arm around kids who weren't as good as him and help them play better."

Chapter 2

'El Capitan'

Va t'en aux etoiles
(Reach for the stars)
Houston Lamar High School motto

AFTER PLAYING MIDDLE-SCHOOL football at St. Michael, Bram wanted to go to public high school to play Big 5A football. Lamar High School was his choice.

"I didn't know how that would go," recalls Dash. "I knew Lamar had a big pool of talent when it came to football. Since Bram was a good baseball player, too, I kind of figured he would end up playing baseball, not football."

Bram was determined to play both sports at Lamar, however. He made the freshman football A-team as backup quarterback and was the starting second baseman on the baseball team. A year later, Bram stepped up his game on the gridiron and became starting quarterback for the varsity.

Tyrone Green, Lamar's former offensive coordinator, remembers his first encounter with Bram, in 2007:

"First time I saw Bram was at fall camp his freshman year.

I'd heard we had a new quarterback coming in from St. Michael's. He was kind of skinny, just an average-looking kid. Once we got started and got him in game situations, we knew he could throw the ball. He was pretty talented.

"He was a bit different in that he was smart, and he was really inquisitive about the plays and everything that was going on. We liked that, but we had another kid, too, and the other kid seemed a little more athletic. Bram was the better passer, though. We just played both, let them compete and battle it out."

Even knowing Bram's athletic talents, Dash wasn't expecting his youngest brother to distinguish himself quite so quickly.

"He was a sophomore on a senior-heavy 5A football team. He didn't have the typical high school quarterback profile; so many are sons of coaches. So, yeah, I was surprised," Dash admitted. "I didn't think he could become the starting quarterback for a big-time high school football team. He was playing with a lot of guys who didn't have many reasons to be patient with a sophomore quarterback. But he did well."

That year, the sophomore kid quarterbacked the Lamar Texans to the second round of the Texas state playoffs.

What quickly jumped off the page about Bram, his coaches observed, was his force of personality, his magnetism with the other players. His teammates flocked around him. Bram almost instantly became the team leader, even volunteering to pick up teammates in his car to bring them to seven-on-seven practice the summer after his freshman season.

"In high school," Dash recalls, "it wasn't that [some of] the kids weren't as good as him." Rather, Dash says, it was Bram's way of relating to each one of his teammates and stepping up into a leadership role that made him stand out.

"The profile of the kids varied dramatically," Dash recalls.

"There were kids who came from private middle schools to play football, others that may have grown up without one of their parents. There were kids from all backgrounds.

"Where I saw him make a difference, during two-a-days he would run a carpool, making sure his teammates could get to practice. On Saturday mornings, he would pick his teammates up and get them to school to get them ready for a game. He has always been very good at relating to everybody and taking care of everybody. His leadership ability is exceptional."

Tyrone Green concurs: "He and his family did a lot of great things for the program. Bram would drive across town to pick up kids. He did things the right way."

"He had a big personality, and it was that way the first time I met him. He was a joker, too. He was always messing with the coaches, hanging around the office. He'd just want to come in, draw up plays, get in the way all the time. We'd have to run him out eventually.

"He was a charmer. He would come late to school, and he'd bring breakfast for the teachers. It was hard to stay irritated with him," Green recalls.

"During his sophomore year he became a very accurate passer. When he was on the field, he just had that 'it' factor. A defensive lineman might be ready to knock the piss out of him, but he'd stand in the pocket and make the play. He was a real tough kid."

Bram continued playing baseball too, both in the infield and as a pitcher, but soon his football and baseball dreams began to collide.

In the fall of his sophomore year, he had been the starting quarterback for every game. As baseball season began, trying to juggle baseball with spring football practice became complicated. The coaches at Lamar asked him to make a choice, the football coach pulling one way, the baseball coach the other. Bram elected to concentrate on football.

Meanwhile, on the Lamar basketball court that year, another superb sophomore athlete, Josh Gordon, was turning heads. Like Bram, he was pulled toward football too. A year later, future NFL star wide receiver Gordon decided to add football to his repertoire, and the Kohlhausen-Gordon tandem took center stage at Houston Lamar.

In their junior and senior years, the pair would lead Lamar to consecutive one-loss regular seasons and into the playoffs. In Bram's three years quarterbacking them, the Texans went 27-7.

One of Bram's Lamar teammates, Zach Mafrige, recalls Bram as the solid rock of the Texans' team.

"The way I explain Bram is, he's a leader. The moment was never too big for him. He never unraveled, no matter what the situation. We looked to him as the go-to guy."

• • •

By the time Bram was a senior, there was little question that he would be one of the state's most highly recruited quarterbacks. He had made improvements in leaps and bounds throughout high school.

"Bram just played really well," recalled former coach Green. You knew right then he had a future as a college quarterback. He had a great delivery. He was accurate, and he learned how to use his legs a little more. He was scrambling better.

"In his senior year, we had a really good team. We had a chance to advance in the playoffs, but he broke his hand the week of our game with Cinco Ranch. The doctors put it in a splint or something, and he couldn't play.

"It really hurt our chances. But he got in the game in the fourth quarter anyway, and it looked like there had never been anything wrong with him. He led us on a late drive where we almost came back to win. It was remarkable what he was able to do. [The broken hand] was [the result of] a bonehead decision, but it was pretty gritty for him to come back and play."

There's nothing unusual about the confluence of bonehead decisions and teen-age boys. Both Bram's mother and his brothers remember the latter part of his high-school years with some ruefulness.

Bram's emergence as a star quarterback in football-crazy Houston had suddenly presented him with all sorts of delightful opportunities. Having been named MVP both his junior and senior years, he was the unquestioned "El Capitan," the head honcho. He had good looks and charisma. Guys wanted to hang out with him. Girls did too.

Did it all go to his head? He was a teen-ager; of course it did.

Looking back on those years, his mother recalls: "At 16, he became a god and didn't love his mother anymore. He didn't think [his parents] knew anything. For a brief period, I was very concerned about him. He resented us even caring about his football, is what I saw."

Gareth had also seen Bram's personality begin to change as his younger brother moved through high school. He was no longer the quiet, somewhat introverted kid who had haunted his big brother's footsteps, wanting to hang out and play ball with Gareth and his friends. It was like watching the rerun of an old movie Gareth had once starred in himself.

"When he started becoming big dog on campus, that's when I saw a change," says Gareth. "He started drinking in high school. He became cocky, aggressive.

"He liked to party and have fun. It runs in the blood in this family."

Dash echoes that assessment:

"We're all very social. That can materialize itself in productive and nonproductive ways. My dad never met a stranger. If he was still around while you were writing this book, you'd have to put aside a week to listen to him. It didn't surprise me that Bram liked to have fun.

"The same reason why he could walk up to a kid from the Fourth Ward, put his arm around him, find something to talk to him about, is the same reason he could go to a party and maybe do some things he shouldn't do.

"We all go through our immature moments. You can't make anybody grow up. They have to do that on their own terms. Sometimes it takes longer than others."

If Bram's coaches were aware of Bram's off-the-field activities, they were equally aware of what he brought to the table as a quarterback and team leader. They were willing to cut the star player a little slack, and "I never saw it affect him in school or playing football," Coach Green recalls.

Never, that is, until the last game of Bram's high-school career.

Lamar had won the district championship, with the playoff game, against Katy's Cinco Ranch, coming up in a week and the state championship an alluring possibility after that.

It was at a post-game party after the district victory that Bram made a major error in judgment. Bram says he was leaving the party when he walked smack into the middle of a dust-up between a teammate and a boy from another school. As Bram remembers it, he swung in defense of his teammate, but the other boy's head was harder than Bram's fist. Bram came away with two fractured knuckles.

It was a costly mistake, both for Bram and for the Texans.

Pacing the sidelines with his hand in a cast during the Texans' playoff game with Cinco Ranch the next week, a desperate and guilt-stricken Bram talked his coaches into putting him in the game, splint and all, late in the fourth quarter. There were only three minutes left, but a touchdown could still win it for the Texans.

"Bram was so cool," recalls Zach Mafrige, who was playing left guard for the Texans. "He ran into the huddle and asked how everyone was doing. He wanted us to know he was ready."

Broken hand throbbing, Bram couldn't handle the pain of taking a snap under center. He was in the shotgun formation for every play, with the Lamar center carefully floating the ball back. Bram marched the Texans down the field, connecting on three successful bubble screen passes for 55 yards. That moved Lamar into scoring position, but with only about a minute and a half left to play the Texans faced a fourth-and-7 situation.

On the premise that the Cinco Ranch defense would be on the alert for another screen, the final play was a fake bubble screen slant underneath. The receiver broke open, but Bram, under heavy pressure, never saw him. Scrambling, he was eventually forced to dump the ball to his tight end, who came up a couple of yards short of the first down.

Game — and high-school career — over.

That failed fourth-down play ended the Texans' dreams of a state championship. Bram knew the Texans would have won the game if he'd been able to play at full capacity. He knew he had let them down, badly.

It would be four years before Bram would throw another punch in anger, but his penchant for playing hard both on and off the field was just getting started.

Chapter 3

'Houston, We Have a Problem'

FROM THE MOMENT he started his freshman year at the University of Houston in 2011, Bram Kohlhausen was a problem, both for the Cougars and for himself.

The root of the problem may have been that Bram had committed to UH in the first place. He could have gone in any number of directions had he waited to commit to a school until after his senior season at Lamar. At least one recruiting service ranked him as the sixth-best high school quarterback in the state of Texas, placing him ahead of such soon-to-be household names as Manziel and Boykin.

But at 17, Bram was thoroughly enjoying his newfound independence. He didn't consult his parents, sought little advice from his older brothers. College was going to be his decision and his decision alone.

"He didn't want us to talk about it," his mother recalls. "He didn't discuss any of the college offers with us."

Bram understood that committing early in his senior season would curtail other potential offers, but Kevin Sumlin had just arrived as the University of Houston's new head coach, and the up-and-coming Kliff Kingsbury, already reputed to be an offensive savant, was the new offensive coordinator.

During recruiting, Kingsbury had told Bram he would be the heir apparent to Cougars' quarterback Case Keenum, who was destined soon to be pitching his passes in the NFL. Together, Sumlin and Kingsbury painted a picture of future national championships at Houston. Eager to be major part of that dream in his hometown, Bram was sold.

"You know how recruiting goes. They promise you the world. Every coach at UH would look me in the eye and tell me they were not going to leave until they were done coaching me. At 18, I believed it, but my parents and brothers didn't. What did they know, right?" Bram recalls ruefully.

"I know my mom wanted me to go to Virginia. And my dad wanted me to go to Utah so he could ski and play golf in the surrounding areas when he visited. It was also about to be Utah's first year in the PAC 12, and that was appealing.

"I never really consulted my brothers about my decision, partially because Gareth was in college, and we didn't really talk that much while he was in school. Dash was married and working 80 hours a week at a law firm. In my own head, I probably thought they didn't care."

They did, of course. Dash wasn't sure that Houston was the best place for Bram. He'd been noticing red flags in Bram's behavior as the big dog at Lamar, and he thought that a new environment, away from home, might help.

He also knew it was a moot point. His little brother wasn't asking for anyone else's opinion.

"His senior year was about his most-difficult-to-deal-with year. He's a high school senior; he thinks he's king of the world. He was close to the vest about his recruiting. He had several Division I schools talking to him that he wouldn't even entertain at the time," Dash recalls.

University of Houston

Bram committed to the University of Houston with two of his high-school teammates. "It was a horrible decision," he says now.

"He wasn't seeking a lot of advice about what to do, despite my best efforts. U of H was by far recruiting him the hardest, and he thought a lot of Kliff. Two other teammates from his high school wanted to go there, so that influenced him as well," Dash says.

So, just after his senior year of classes had begun, in August 2010, Bram made a spur-of-the-moment decision.

"I don't remember the specific day," Bram says, "but I went to school not knowing I was going to commit that day. I was sitting in class, and two of my teammates texted me and said they were going to commit to UH that day. I had a major fear of missing out, so I went and committed with them.

"It was a horrible decision, considering how many schools I had recruiting me at the time. It turned them all away. My recruiting process was essentially over once I committed, because no coach was going to waste his time trying to get a kid already committed to his hometown school to flip his decision. At the time I committed I had offers from Houston, Virginia and Utah, and on signing day North Carolina offered me, because [quarterback] Everett Golson flipped to Notre Dame."

Initially, Bill and Donna Kohlhausen were thrilled that Bram would be playing so close to home. They could easily watch his home games. He could drop by for dinner occasionally, bring home his laundry. They would still be involved in his life.

"We were delighted when he went to U of H," says Donna, "but it was the wrong route to go. He wanted to go there because of Kliff Kingsbury. I think he had a man crush. Then suddenly Kingsbury was gone, and he ended up with a coach who didn't know anything."

Redshirted as a freshman, Bram would have just one fall with Sumlin and Kingsbury as his coaches. Having leveraged the Cougars' 13-1 2011 season into a lucrative offer from Texas A&M, they were gone to greener pastures, where Kingsbury would spend a year developing "Johnny Football" Manziel before becoming head man at Texas Tech.

The new head coach at the University of Houston was Tony Levine, fresh out of Purdue University.

"You may not remember him," Bram said. "Nobody does."

• • •

The whole University of Houston interlude was to be a regrettable chapter in Bram's life, and not all of that had to do with the coaching. Another highly recruited quarterback, David Piland out of Southlake Carroll, had also arrived on campus. Bram was quickly learning what thousands of college football players have learned over the years: A new coaching staff feels no obligation to honor a previous coach's promises. Bram soon found himself not just behind Keenum but also looking up at Piland on the depth chart.

As a redshirt, Bram was suddenly at loose ends. He wasn't making road trips with the team on weekends, wasn't getting many practice reps. His focus wavered, began to shift away from football.

"I kind of checked out that year," Bram says of his freshman season. "Since I wasn't traveling, I spent most weekends with friends in Austin. I started not showing up to lift weights, didn't watch extra film, didn't spend a lot of time with the coaches. I still balled out on the field during practice. My teammates loved me. But I wasn't as mature then as I should have been."

Kingsbury remembers Bram as being ultra-talented but a bit unfocused during their one season together at Houston. He knew Bram had natural ability from what he'd seen of him at Lamar:

"He was a really natural thrower. I was very impressed with how he could spin the ball, the way it came out, smooth release, very effortless. You could tell it came easy, throwing the ball.

"As a freshman at Houston, he got to watch Case Keenum operate, but football wasn't No. 1 on his priority list at that time. He didn't work as hard as we would have liked, but guys still liked him. I thought he definitely had the ability. He's a smart kid but maybe didn't apply himself as well as he could have. I thought he could be a big-time player."

After the departure of Sumlin and Kingsbury, the disappointment at UH was palpable, and Bram's unhappiness and frustration with his personal situation made matters even worse for him. Now, he says, he realizes he just wasn't mature enough to understand that he was at least partially responsible for his own predicament.

Doug Meacham, who would play a pivotal role in Bram's eventual landing at TCU, arrived in the spring of 2012 as Levine's new offensive coordinator. By that time, there was no longer any doubt: Bram Kohlhausen had mentally checked out of football.

"I remember Coach Meacham scheduling an 8 o'clock quarterbacks meeting that spring," Bram says. "I had a 9 a.m. tee time. He was late, didn't show up until 8:30 or so. By then, I'd been gone for 15 minutes. I just told the other guys to tell me what he said.

"The next day he said, 'What the f*ck? We had a meeting yesterday!' I told him I had a tee time.

"If I could, I would do some things differently. I had too many friends (in Houston), and they'd want to go play golf, so I'd skip the voluntary seven-on-seven drill. Or I'd leave town to go party."

It wasn't just the coaches who were noticing Bram's less-than-stellar attitude toward practice. Victor Ignatiev was an assistant equipment manager at UH, a post he would hold later at TCU. Coming from rival Houston high schools — Bram from Lamar, Victor from Bellaire — they quickly became friends.

"He was like any typical freshman coming in," Ignatiev recalls, "thinking they can play, they can start, they belong in the NFL. At some point, reality sets in. He had had some accolades coming out of high school. I think he'd been ranked something like the 30th-best quarterback in the country when he came to Houston.

"He started on the scout team, but he didn't take it very seriously. He was like, 'Well, I'm in my hometown, I've got friends, I've got parties to go to, I'm in college now, I'm a big-time college quarterback.' I'm thinking, 'You're just a backup. You're really nothing special.' The guy he had in front of him was good enough, so Bram wasn't going to play anytime soon," Ignatiev says.

That wasn't the way Bram saw it back in 2012, though: "I thought I should be the starter, but that spring I was having some sore-arm issues and I still wasn't as committed as I should have been. Still, I thought I definitely outperformed Piland in spring camp and in the fall. But I stayed second-team."

And things were about to get worse. By midway through the 2012 season, senior Crawford Jones was backing up Piland, and Bram had slipped to third team. He would see little game action, mopping up against Alabama-Birmingham and throwing two interceptions in an embarrassing 72-42 loss to SMU.

Dash was in the stands for that wretched SMU game, watching as Piland suffered a concussion early in the game. Jones, another redshirt player, had finished the first half, and Bram started the second half, though he'd had few reps that week and was ill-prepared. It wasn't pretty.

"Bram was like a deer in the headlights," Dash recalls. "He didn't know the plays. He was calling the previous season's plays. He threw like three pick-sixes [actually, only two, both on screen passes, matching the number of interceptions that Piland and Jones had each also thrown]. That got my attention because he looked terrible, and I didn't know why. He never played again that season."

Already behind Piland on the depth chart during the previous spring, Bram watched helplessly as Levine and the new coaching staff brought in their own recruits before the 2013 season. They included highly rated quarterbacks John O'Korn out of Florida and Tyler's Greg Ward, who would eventually go on to an NFL career as a wide receiver.

Gareth knew that all these developments added up to big trouble for Bram's playing time. He wanted to see Bram out of UH so badly that he even bet his little brother $1,000 that Bram wouldn't leave. He figured it would be money well spent if Bram ended up accepting the challenge and transferring somewhere else to play football.

After O'Korn and Ward arrived on campus for the 2013 season, Dash went out to watch a scrimmage during the team's two-a-day practices at fall camp. Bram got to run only one series, fewest of any of the four quarterbacks. He was clearly now behind not only Piland but Ward and O'Korn as well.

"I told him. 'Look, you're not playing here. There's no way. The coach has no reason to play you. The one time he put you in was an epic failure.'

"That was the impetus for Bram to start thinking about transferring out. That's when I got more involved. He was like, 'How the hell do you get to a junior college?' I started calling people; he started calling people."

From that point, things moved quickly, Bram recalls.

"We started school [at UH] on a Monday with a game scheduled in two weeks," Bram says. "On the Friday before the game, I told Levine I was transferring, and within a few days I was in California, looking for junior colleges."

The next thing Dash knew, Bram was telling him about Los Angeles Harbor College: "Bram called me and said the coach from the previous year had left and taken all his players with him. They had a whole new team."

Chapter 4

A California Reality Check

BRAM AND HIS MOTHER Donna hopped on a flight to L.A. Bill Kohlhausen did the hard part, driving Bram's car to the West Coast from Houston, a grueling trip of more than 1,500 miles. No one knew, of course, that Bill had only two years left to live. At that moment, the family's focus was entirely on Bram.

"California made a big difference," says Donna Kohlhausen. "When Bram came home from UH after quitting, he came through the front door and literally fell into my arms bawling. It was family time. Dash came over. Everybody had to be here for moral support.

"Going out to California, I think he realized how much his parents cared and were doing for him. We spent some bucks doing it, including getting him an apartment at Redondo Beach."

For new Los Angeles Harbor College Seahawks coach Reuben Ale, who was in the process of trying to get the school's football program back on its feet, landing a quarterback the caliber of Bram Kohlhausen was an unexpected godsend. He had been desperately hunting down prospective quarterbacks without much success when he got the call saying that Bram wanted to go the JUCO route, with the goal of having a good season so that he could springboard off it to hook up with another four-year school.

"I tried to talk him out of it," Ale recalled, "pointing out that four-year scholarships are hard to come by and that, as much as I would like to have him, I wasn't really comfortable taking him away from Houston.

"I was a new coach at the time, had just taken over from the previous coach and staff. We did a little background check, and we knew he was legit. We knew he would be our guy.

"I told Bram we were trying to rebuild the program and if he wanted to be a part of it, he was welcome to come out to California. The moment he stepped off the plane I told him he was our starting quarterback. I just thought he was very polished. For him to come down from a four-year school to a junior college didn't make sense. But he said he just wanted to compete. He wanted a new start."

Ale had no problem selling Bram on the California lifestyle. And seeing him in action in Bram's first practice only confirmed the lucky break that had just dropped into Ale's lap:

"He came in and we called a couple of deep throws, and it was 'Wow! This is a big-time quarterback.' We had a couple of guys who could do some things athletic-wise, so we ran them on a couple of routes. Bram would put it right on the money."

• • •

Los Angeles Harbor College sits at the intersection of Interstate 110 and the Pacific Highway, with the neighborhoods of Carson and Compton just to the east and the more affluent Rolling Hills and Palos Verdes to the west. The school is a member of the South Coast Conference of the

California Community College Athletic Association. With 108 schools in 10 conferences in its jurisdiction, the CCCAA has a reputation for producing some of best junior college football players in the country.

Bram, however, wasn't impressed. The downgrade in the caliber of talent and milieu was a rude awakening, especially with the Seahawks amid a rebuild:

"I was shocked in the sense that it was pretty much high school ball all over again. The kids didn't respect the coaches. They'd show up late to meetings, late to practice, argue and even challenge the coaches to fight. Just a lot of immaturity. They were so immature they wouldn't shower after practice or games.

"The coaches were very military-style. They would yell and kick kids out of practice. There were a lot of ups and downs. Some of the coaching techniques were terrible, but at the end of the day it was sort of a business trip for me, so I just kept my head down, trying to graduate and hope for a D1 scholarship.

"A lot of the players were also OK with losing. I remember playing the first game and there were maybe 30 people in the stands. It was tough. Honestly, though, it was a great experience, very humbling. I hope I was able to teach some of those kids how you are supposed to conduct yourself as a D1 athlete."

For Bram, L.A. Harbor was a far cry from the football dream he had been pursuing, but it provided an emotional and mental reset that had been a long time coming.

The in-your-face dose of reality forced him to reflect on his own life and the immaturity he'd displayed at the University of Houston. Without his family and his usual posse around him, he curtailed the partying, concentrating on football and on school — and on learning, for the first time, to be truly independent.

"I was always concerned for him," Dash recalls. "He liked to party, but I never put him on the same level as a Johnny Manziel or some of these other kids. I wasn't concerned for him in the sense of 'You're going to kill yourself or kill someone else.' I thought he was a little irresponsible and reckless, but I didn't think he was out of control.

"I know that he did a lot of growing up when he left Houston. If my son is ever in a position between staying home and going elsewhere, I would encourage him to go elsewhere. It was too easy for Bram to get in his car, drive home, get his laundry done, all that stuff.

"He learned how to take care of himself out there in California. I think he realized very quickly what he'd left, both on the football field and the situation at home. Leaving U of H and going through that turned out to be the best thing for him."

What didn't go so well was the actual football, though this was no fault of Bram's. The team may have been struggling, but Bram himself got off to a good start, winning conference offensive player of the week after he went 28-for-38 for 280 yards and two touchdowns in his junior college debut. That LAHC had been blown out 50-19 by Cerritos in that game just made the honor even more remarkable.

The Seahawks were also trounced, 48-17, by Golden West College at Orange Coast in the season's second game, but again Bram played well, hitting 26 of 41 passes for 264 yards and another pair of TDs. In his third game, he had hit six of his first 10 passes against Ventura in the first half when he went down on his left side and one of his own offensive linemen fell on top of him. He felt his left shoulder pop out.

He practiced little the following week but started the fourth game anyway. Playing from behind and trying to throw a Hail Mary, Bram took another hit to the left shoulder and again felt it pop out.

He was done for the season.

Coach Ale would call Bram's season-ending injury "the saddest thing I've seen in all my years of coaching." Four weeks later, Bram had surgery to repair a labrum tear in his left shoulder.

"Bram called me in tears," Dash says; "he didn't know what he was going to do. His filmed appearances [at Houston] were terrible. It wasn't pretty. He'd had a couple of good games at L.A. Harbor, but nobody was going to give him credit for that. I was concerned, but I told him, whatever he did, he had to graduate from that junior college — that that was the most important thing now."

Donna Kohlhausen flew out for the surgery and stayed with Bram long enough to be sure he was off the pain pills. A medical marijuana prescription, Bram would say later, helped immensely. Meanwhile, he continued to study and attend classes, intent on graduating from LAHC.

"After the surgery I basically just went to rehab for my shoulder and to class," Bram says. "I stopped attending practice and games. I flew back to Texas a lot. The coaches, the administrators, everyone was great. They helped me take the correct classes to graduate in three months."

Bram's entire L.A. sojourn had lasted only from Aug. 25 to Dec. 3, 2013. He had graduated, but his hopes for a comeback season that might attract the attention of another four-year school had been torpedoed by the shoulder injury.

What was next? Was it time to forget about football and move on with his life?

Chapter 5
Seeing Purple

IT WAS OBVIOUS to Dash Kohlhausen after Bram's interlude at Los Angeles Harbor College that his youngest brother had gone through a major change in attitude. For the first time since graduating from high school, he was no longer operating as if playing college football was his God-given right. He'd dropped his big-time-football-star demeanor. He'd been humbled; he feared that the shoulder surgery might mark the end of his playing career.

He was so distraught after the injury, in fact, that Dash initially "felt like shit" for having pushed Bram to travel to California to try to salvage what was left of his college career. Then he realized what the experience had done for Bram: His little brother, almost 12 years his junior, had finally grown up.

"I don't know that he ever grew up until he went through this U of H and junior college process," Dash says. "Look at Johnny Manziel: When you're *the guy* and there's nobody behind you, it's easy to make bad decisions. But in college, everybody around you can play. Being on the same team with Case Keenum was very good for Bram. Watching guys who he thought weren't as good as him pass him up was a learning experience for him. Understanding that football wasn't a right was good for him.

"A lot of guys would have just quit playing, joined a fraternity and enjoyed themselves. That part is something I've always been proud of him for. He found a reason to stick it out. Here he was, never having started a game in his college career; then to get to that bowl game and pull off what he did was remarkable."

Getting there, though, wouldn't be easy. Bram first had to hope that some major college program would look past his crash and burn at Houston and his record of less than three full games at L.A. Harbor.

What Bram had on his side was his ability to relate to people, to charm them with his engaging personality and impress them with his sincerity. Yes, he had a reputation as a guy who might enjoy himself off the field a bit too much now and again. But he was also known as a straight shooter — an intelligent, coachable quarterback and an exceptional teammate in the locker room. He'd obviously learned a few life lessons at Houston and on the West Coast. He was willing to take whatever role he could get on whatever team that would have him.

For a brief time, that team looked like it might be the Big Daddy of them all in the Lone Star state — the University of Texas. Bram Kohlhausen in burnt orange? TCU fans might cringe at the thought today, but it's where he would have landed if the Longhorns had offered him even a walk-on opportunity.

"There had been all these rumors that I was going to wind up at UT," Bram says. "My photo was even on the cover of [the Longhorn fan publication] *Orangebloods* on the eve of signing day. I thought, 'This is how bad things are at Texas;

they're talking about a junior college guy instead of four-star recruits.' "

Dash chimes in: "It all starts with the whole Texas debacle. It's funny the way bad things turned into good things. Charlie Strong was coming in at UT. They were thin at quarterback. Bram was talking to someone there, and there was some discussion about him walking on.

"An L.A. reporter called and was interviewing him for a story about junior-college quarterbacks. It somehow got reported that Bram might be walking on at UT. It gets picked up nationally."

It didn't take long for that report to be scotched. Late on the same day of the *L.A. Daily News* report, the *Austin American-Statesman*'s online Longhorn site *Hook 'Em* reported:

For those getting worked up over reports this morning that former Houston Cougars quarterback Bram Kohlhausen will walk on at Texas this fall, not so fast.

Kohlhausen, contacted by the American-Statesman, *said the* Los Angeles Daily News *report today is not accurate.*

"UT hasn't given me a promise of any walk-on spot yet. We are in communication, but there hasn't been any promise or anything," Kohlhausen said. "We are talking, but there is no decision made by either side."

"Needless to say," Dash says," UT never called back."

• • •

Fortuitously, Doug Meacham had just arrived at TCU from Houston as the Horned Frogs' co-offensive coordinator alongside Sonny Cumbie, under head coach Gary Patterson. Though Bram knew he'd let Meacham down at Houston, the two still had forged a good relationship.

"I called Coach Meacham and told him I needed a place to play," Bram says. "I was just reaching out to coaches I knew. I didn't know if TCU had a place for me or not. But Coach

Meacham told me to come out during spring practice to visit. My dad and I drove out there.

"We watched practice, got a tour, met Coach Cumbie, met Coach Patterson briefly. Coach Meacham said during the tour, 'We've got a spot for you if you want, but you'll have to walk on,' " Bram recalls.

"I thought it would be a good transition for him," Meacham says. "I showed Sonny some clips of him, and he said, 'Bring him in.' "

Meacham had little to lose. At that point, TCU coaches weren't sure what they had in the multi-talented but often erratic Trevone Boykin, who could rack up spectacular stats but whose first two seasons had produced as many downs as ups. Boykin was the only quarterback TCU had returning, so depth was definitely needed, and Bram was one way to provide that.

"We knew he had arm talent and that he had tons of experience in our offense at Houston and junior college," Cumbie recalls. "There was talent, knowledge, a certain sense of calmness that he brought as a senior. He threw the ball really well, got the ball out of his hand quick, threw a pretty ball. He could spin it. His decision-making could get him in trouble, and that might have come from an overconfidence in his abilities.

"We felt he could exceed expectations, depending on how he took to the coaching, a guy who could operate the offense in a backup role. His demeanor on the sidelines, in the locker room — he was never sour about anything. When you leave a place like Houston and go the junior college route, there's a certain sense of humility that settles in."

For Bram and his family, after so many disappointments over the last two years, any opportunity for him to continue to play major college football was a godsend. That it would be at a high-caliber, fast-rising program like TCU's, with its solid academic reputation, was a priceless bonus.

"I told Bram to take Meacham's offer and run with it," Dash says. "It was going to be the best offer he was going to get, and getting a degree from TCU would be great.

"It's almost like taboo to talk about it, but player recruiting and coaches' hirings are so much about relationships and not about talent. I think that's where Bram can make an impression on somebody.

"I coached Little League baseball for over 10 years. I always told my kids, if you show up late to work at 10:30 every day, it matters. If you're the first person there at 8 o'clock, it matters. If you see your boss at the grocery store, go over and shake his hand.

"That's where Bram shines. The people he meets love him. Kevin Sumlin used to live around the corner from us. Even though he was with Bram for only a year [as head coach at UH], and with all the great quarterbacks he's had, he still loves Bram. He just makes a great impression.

"Doug Meacham didn't want him [just] because he threw a great football. It was because he knew he was a good guy and that he would come in and do the right thing."

Bill Kohlhausen, just months away from a diagnosis of cancer that would become terminal, didn't want to see Bram miss this opportunity either. He told his son he'd foot the bills — what would amount to nearly $90,000 for the semesters Bram wasn't on scholarship — if TCU was where his son wanted to be.

"It was definitely a big upgrade from U of H," Bram recalls. "At Houston, nobody cared about their athletics. It was a commuter school. There was no campus life. Nobody came to the games unless we were ranked or 8-0.

"Everybody at TCU lives and breathes TCU football and

baseball. At Houston, we were just in the shadows of so many other major sports venues.

"Yeah, I was impressed. TCU was the first to offer me a spot, and my dad was willing to pay for it. So I jumped on the opportunity and forgot about Texas."

• • •

As always, Bram quickly made friends with his new teammates.

Charlie Reid, a redshirt freshman tight end from Fort Worth All Saints, was one of those new teammates who was impressed with the new arrival.

"When you see him, you don't immediately think he's a quarterback," Reid says. "He's not a huge guy, but he's such a gamer. He may be the most competitive guy I've ever met in my life. He's a clutch-time player with a dog-eat-dog mentality. He was a fun football player to watch.

"Bram would be playing dominoes, and he'd get fired up if he wasn't winning. I remember being involved in a three-on-three charity basketball league, and his team went all the way to the championship. He was balls-to-the-wall."

Though Boykin was (and is still) the only TCU player in history to post 200 yards passing, 100 yards rushing and 100 yards receiving in the same game in his freshman season, Bram also knew that Boykin and Casey Pachall had co-quarterbacked the Frogs to a miserable 4-8 record in 2013. Boykin had even been moved to wide receiver late in the season, attempting just two total passes in the last two games.

Boykin was the only quarterback with any experience returning in 2014. Bram, always confident, looked at the stat sheet and figured he could beat Boykin out to become the starter. Then, two weeks after the Frogs' 2014 spring game, after Bram had agreed to walk on as a junior, came the announcement that Matt Joeckel was transferring to TCU. The

TCU

TCU's quarterback crew in a festive mood during the 2015 holiday season, from left: redshirt freshman Foster Sawyer; No. 2 QB Bram Kohlhausen; quarterbacks coach Sonny Cumbie; Texas A&M transfer Kenny Hill (who would succeed Boykin in 2016); third-team freshman Grayson Muehlstein; TCU star QB Trevone Boykin; offensive analyst Hudson Fuller.

highly recruited Arlington High star had just graduated from Texas A&M but had a year of eligibility remaining, and he wanted to play his final season at a school that could offer him a chance to start.

"Everybody thought Joeckel would be our starting quarterback," Bram recalls, "but Trevone just had an amazing fall camp. I was looking at third string. Meacham kept telling me everything was open. That entire fall l think I got three reps. Everyone's mind was made up.

"At that point, I was 21. I was just trying to hang on and be the third-string guy. I didn't think I'd be getting any of the reps with the ones and twos."

Then, "after fall camp, Coach Cumbie told me I was the fourth-string quarterback, and I didn't understand why. I was better than the guy who was third string," freshman Zach Allen.

"For half a season I was third string; then, at Texas Tech,

Matt blew out his knee.

"Zach and I went back and forth at No. 2, but by the end of the season I was playing well and wound up as the backup for the Peach Bowl. We blew out Ole Miss, and I played seven or eight minutes in the fourth quarter, basically just handing it off with a screen pass now and then."

Off the field, Bram fit right into his teammates' party scene — and there were plenty of wins to celebrate.

"My junior year at TCU was pretty tame when it came to drugs," he recalls, "but the alcohol never stopped flowing. After every win a group of us had a routine: Following our Sunday practice, knowing we didn't practice Mondays, we would go get pizza, then go straight to the strip club in Fort Worth, spending way too much money every week. We literally went every single week.

"We partied harder on Sundays than we did on Saturdays because we didn't practice on Mondays. So there was justification. And I was a backup to a Heisman candidate, so I didn't feel important."

Far from resenting his top rival, Bram had by that time become fast friends with Boykin, even rooming with him. Bram no longer fantasized about becoming TCU's starting quarterback. There was a reason the job belonged to Boykin: He was not just good; he was often spectacular.

"Once you saw his arm strength and ability to run and how smart he was as a football player . . . he knows matchups, spacing, he knows the game. There was no question he was the best quarterback on the roster. He was a Heisman-caliber athlete," Bram says of his former teammate.

Boykin loved the nightlife, though. He couldn't walk into a saloon anywhere near campus and not have a bar full of free drinks stacked up in front of him. And the night before the Peach Bowl in Atlanta, Bram literally rode to Trevone's rescue.

Not on a horse, of course — in an Uber.

That night in Georgia, on his way back to the team hotel to make curfew, Bram got a text telling him some of his teammates, including Boykin, were still partying at a club and were thinking of staying there until closing time.

That, Bram knew, would not lead to a happy ending. Although he knew it would mean breaking curfew himself, Bram instructed his Uber driver to turn around and directed the car to the club. Once there, he ushered Boykin and five more of his teammates, all starters, into the Uber and hustled them back to the hotel.

They didn't get back into their rooms until an hour after curfew. If any of the coaches noticed their absence, no one said anything.

Dash recalled the way his brother put himself on the line for his fellow quarterback in Atlanta as a demonstration of Bram's extraordinary loyalty to Boykin.

"My point is, the bond between those two guys was surprisingly strong. After the [Alamo Bowl] game, the first thing Bram was talking about was Trevone Boykin. You have to understand their relationship to understand why he would do that.

"Bram knew that Tre was the better player, but he also knew that he [Bram] had been dealt a better deal in life. He just has a knack of being able to put his arm around people and of being a leader in a way that few backup quarterbacks are."

Chapter 6

A Devastating Blow

MEANWHILE, BACK IN HOUSTON, Donna Kohlhausen wasn't particularly enjoying Bram's stay at TCU. She was accustomed to seeing her son playing, even starring, on the field, not standing on the sidelines with a clipboard.

That didn't mean she and Bill didn't show up for the home games in Fort Worth, of course.

"It was really frustrating for me," Donna says. "I dreaded going to the games. Bill had to be there for everything, even Frog Walk [from dorm to stadium], two hours before the game. It meant so much to him to see Bram doing the Frog Walk.

"Bill would then go get some popcorn and sit in the stands, watching Bram warm up. That was his game. It meant so much to him. I'm not sure towards the end, after the radiation, that he even knew which one Bram was."

Bram's 2014 junior season at TCU had been relatively uneventful until that terrible day in October when his mom phoned to tell him that his dad had been diagnosed with melanoma.

Doctors initially pegged Bill's cancer somewhere between Stage 1 and Stage 2. There was optimism that, with treatment, he could eventually beat it.

Instead, it was the beginning of the end. Thirteen months later, Bill Kohlhausen would be gone.

"It was an extremely painful year, especially being away from my dad in Fort Worth, trying to focus on football. I would only get the filtered-down version of what was really happening because the family wanted me to concentrate on football. I never knew how sick he really was or shared the experience of spending days in hospital waiting rooms.

"I think I was trying to ignore it, maybe going out at night more than I should. I didn't really talk to anybody about it. I was so removed from the situation. My brothers would take him to the doctor's office. They saw him at his worst. My brothers were the real troopers who were there for him, hands-on.

"I only saw him at his worst one time, back at home, and that was the last time I ever saw my father. On my way back to Fort Worth after that, I cried the entire four-hour drive, knowing I had a season to get back to and that was the last time I would ever see him.

"At that time the cancer had spread to his brain, and he couldn't even speak, so I was only able to talk to him hoping he could process what I was saying. His appetite never changed, so we sat on our porch and crushed Marble Slab ice cream together."

In August 2015, doctors told the family that Bill didn't have much time left, maybe only weeks. Dash and Gareth hurriedly made plans to take their parents to TCU's 2015 season-opener at the University of Minnesota.

"There were multiple nights my senior season I would get bad news, break down crying with my girlfriend at the time, then resort to getting blackout drunk to cope," Bram recalls.

"I don't think it affected me on the field or at practice at all, because any good athlete is able to tunnel their emotions and lock in for a couple hours. When you are on the field, nothing else really matters."

It was when Bram was off the field that the pain cascaded over him again, drowning out everything else.

"I feel like my emotions were so up and down during my entire college career," Bram says. At TCU, "I partied all during my junior season with alcohol, then when spring came around, I knew I had to straighten up to win my second-string quarterback battle with [redshirt freshman] Foster Sawyer.

"After winning the second-string spot both in spring and fall, the partying picked up again.

"A lot of the time guys like to smoke weed – which I think is healthier than drinking – and watch a movie to kill the time between meetings, practice, classes and games. Our athletic director [Chris Del Conte] told our team that they were going to crack down on drug testing, so that year a lot of people resorted to drinking.

"With the weight of my dad's sickness and again being a backup, I was drinking four or five times a week. I was reaping the benefits of hanging with Tre, where kids at school would buy us shots or drinks the entire night.

"When my dad's sickness started getting really bad and I was told he would not be attending any more games because he was too sick, I resorted to a lot of alcohol, anything that would help drown out the fact that my dad was dying and there was nothing I could do about it. It was going out all night on Thursdays and making it through walk-through and meetings on Fridays using Listerine strips and tobacco. Then on Saturdays I'd get an IV before the games to hydrate."

The solace Bram could never quite chase down in the bars he discovered instead on the football field. There he could focus only on the game and what he did best. Football was his sanctuary, and it didn't matter that Boykin was the undisputed No. 1 going into spring camp in 2015. Bram's clear mission was to remain No. 2.

• • •

To hold onto that backup job, Bram faced a head-to-head competition with Sawyer, who had been rated the No. 2 quarterback recruit in Texas and 13th nationally coming out of Fort Worth All Saints in 2014.

Bram's status as a walk-on kept him on edge, put a chip on his shoulder. He swallowed his pride and kept quiet, but inside he felt the sting of being underappreciated.

"Foster was either a four- or five-star recruit, depending on what service you looked at. He was also on scholarship, and I wasn't. The coaches were looking for reasons to make him the backup quarterback."

Bram and Foster would compete throughout the spring of 2015 and go at it again during fall camp. But Bram held onto the No. 2 spot behind Boykin.

It was Bram's steadiness that kept him there, Cumbie notes:

"We let Foster have some reps and tried to challenge him a little bit, but Bram's consistency just won the backup job going into that season. It was a thing that helped in our quarterbacks' room, where we had an obvious starter and we had guys who understood their roles."

Trevone Boykin agrees: "We practiced together every day. I saw the ability. Bram was very smart. He could retain information. He always had the ability to throw the ball, and we knew that in our quarterbacks room. I think some people fell asleep on that."

With Boykin playing at such a high level – he would complete almost 65 percent of his passes, for more than 3,500 yards and 31 TDs in 2015 – there was little need for a backup except for two key Big 12 games after Boykin suffered an ankle injury. Overall in 2015, Bram would see action in just five games, completing a more-than-respectable 55 of 88 passes (62 percent) for 720 yards and one touchdown.

Cumbie had casually mentioned to Bram before the 2015 season began that they needed to put him on scholarship, since he was the clear backup quarterback, but as the season wore on, there was no follow-through. Bram, not wanting to rock the boat, didn't bring it up again.

"I thought I was going to get [a scholarship] my entire senior year," Bram recalls. "But I never resented it. It was just a little insulting. Everybody in the entire program knew I was a scholarship player."

If Bill Kohlhausen, once a prominent Houston tort attorney, had been well, he likely would have told his son to push harder for that scholarship. Preoccupied with his father's illness, Bram had shrugged and let it slide. The money, fortunately, wasn't an issue for his family, and Bram was grateful to finish out his football career in a major college program. TCU had become home, and Bram loved the life of a college football player. Sometimes, by his own admission, maybe too much.

• • •

The worst day of Bram's young life came on Nov. 7, in Stillwater, Okla., home of the Oklahoma State Cowboys, and it had nothing to do with football or anything that would happen on the field. He was awakened before dawn on game day by the phone call he had long been dreading: Bram's brother Gareth broke the news to his little brother that their dad had died.

Bill Kohlhausen's last real glimpse of his son on a football field had come five weeks earlier, when Bram made a cameo appearance in TCU's 50-7 rout of Texas in early October.

Having known that his father's death was coming, and would be a mercy, didn't ease the pain that crushed Bram that day. Along with the hollow, empty feeling of devastating loss, there was also guilt, both because he felt he hadn't been there for his dad and because now he felt he wouldn't be there for his teammates.

"I put a lot of blame on myself for us losing the Oklahoma State game," Bram says. "We were on the road, and I was Trevone's roommate. I remember it was a day game, so meetings and breakfast started around 8 a.m. I found out that my dad had passed away at like 5 that morning.

"I was bawling, crying my eyes out, and that woke up Tre, our starting quarterback who clearly needed rest for a huge game on the road against Oklahoma State. I knew this, so I took a shower, and that probably kept him up, too. Then I went and woke up Coach Cumbie, our quarterbacks' coach, who also needed his sleep to call plays. I felt like I was a distraction while crying during the entire pre-game meetings and bus ride to the stadium."

Sparked by quarterback Mason Rudolph's 352-yard, five-touchdown performance, No. 14 Oklahoma State upset No. 8 TCU 49-29 that day. It's a very unhappy memory for Cumbie, and not just because of the loss on the field. He wanted so badly to be able to say something to help ease Bram's pain.

"There's no handbook on how to handle that situation," Cumbie says. "Personally, when you see kids who have been great teammates and then they go through personal adversity, you just want to help them so badly.

"We really wanted him to play against Kansas and to finish the job against Oklahoma, just because on a personal level you wanted to see him have something to feel good about.

"Then," says Cumbie, skipping forward to the Alamo Bowl, "to see it happen on an even bigger stage, in that bowl game, that's what makes coaching worthwhile, to see a kid battle through that."

• • •

Bram spent the week after the Oklahoma State game back in Houston with family, attending his dad's memorial service. He missed the entire week of practice but returned to TCU in time for the home game against Kansas on Saturday, Nov. 14. Late in the first quarter Boykin suffered an ankle injury. Bram, not having taken a practice rep all week, trotted onto the field.

Surprisingly, considering his all-too-recent loss and his lack of preparation, he played remarkably well, completing 13 of 19 first-half passes for 112 yards. Just after halftime, though, he threw a critical interception. It was enough for Meacham and Cumbie, who understood how emotionally fragile Bram had to be, to send freshman Sawyer in at quarterback.

Sawyer struggled, completing just one of his seven pass attempts, but that single completion resulted in a dramatic 60-yard touchdown that helped TCU eke out a win, 23-17.

The next week, with 18th-ranked TCU facing No. 7 Oklahoma on the road and Boykin still recovering, Sawyer was bumped up ahead of Bram to start against the Sooners.

"They made that decision that week even before practice," Bram recalls. "I had the best practices I'd ever had that week. I think they put him in a bad position — freshman, OU on the road. Why not start the guy who won the second-team job in practice?"

The game was indeed too big for the inexperienced Sawyer, who threw three interceptions. After the last one in the third quarter, the Sooners were leading 30-13 and Bram finally got his chance. The TCU offense, stymied all day without Boykin and injured No. 1 receiver Josh Doctson, suddenly came to life.

"We had two drives that weren't very good," Bram says. Then we came out deep in our own end of the field and ran a play we'd worked on all week. It went for an 86-yard touchdown to KaVontae Turpin."

The Frogs' long touchdown rattled the Sooners. A 43-yard TCU field goal by Jaden Oberkrom cut OU's lead to 30-23. With 51 seconds left, TCU's Emanuel Porter outleaped two defenders in the right corner of the end zone to pull down a 14-yard touchdown pass from Bram on a fade route. It was 30-29. TCU could kick to tie and send the game into overtime or go for two to win it.

Overtime must have been tempting, since OU starting quarterback Baker Mayfield hadn't returned after a head-to-head hit by TCU's Ty Summers in the first quarter, and backup QB Trevor Knight was struggling. But Sooners running back Samaje Perine was routinely slashing through the Frogs' defense, including a 72-yard touchdown run.

TCU coach Gary Patterson had gone for the 2-point conversion after a 26-yard Aaron Green touchdown run earlier in the game, and that attempt had failed. Had he opted for a successful kick at that point, the game would have been tied with only one point need for a TCU win.

Now, though, Patterson stayed true to his strategy: Play for the tie at home; play for the win on the road. He doubled down and opted for the knockout punch, waving Bram back onto the field to try to win the game outright with less than a minute to play.

The 2-point conversion play called for an out pattern on the left and a "jig" route – Turpin would fake a corner, then run a post – also from the left. Bram dropped back, watching for Turpin's cut. But OU defensive end Eric Striker broke through the protection, lunging at Bram's ankles. The sudden pressure flushed Bram out of the pocket just as Turpin cut inside. Bram stepped up and around Striker and rolled to his right.

Bram would realize later, after watching the tape, that he had bailed too soon, that he should have just stepped up to give Turpin time to run his route. Instead, sprinting right and with Sooner defenders coming up to meet him, Bram kept his eye on Turpin, now flashing toward the right corner of the end zone but quickly closing in on the sideline.

Bram tried to flip the ball up and over onrushing OU safety Steven Parker, but he failed to get enough air on it. Parker timed his leap perfectly to swat the pass down and end the Frogs' rally one point short. Oklahoma prevailed, 30-29.

What still troubles Bram, though, is the play he didn't call.

"The play I should have run was 'quarterback power,' what we called Scuba. We'd been told all week that, if they showed an empty box, to run the quarterback power, whatever the situation. That's exactly what they did. But I didn't have enough confidence to change the play, and having brought us that far back, I didn't want to blow it. So I went with the play that was called. If I had audibled to the quarterback power, I would have scored, and we would have won.

"That was probably my favorite game. If we'd have come back to win there, beat OU, which was top 10 at the time, who knows what would have happened? We probably would have been in a playoff situation."

Later, someone would text Bram a screenshot from behind the offense looking into the end zone. In the photo, there's not a defender in sight behind the two defensive tackles. One of the tackles is lined up between TCU's center and left guard. The other is spread a little wider, between the right guard and right tackle.

Between the K and the second O in the big white "O-K-L-A-H-O-M-A" emblazoned in the end zone — a gaping space of at least 10 yards — the sender has drawn a large red rectangle enclosing the words, "THERE IS NOBODY HERE."

"I should have called Scuba-P," Bram says again. "The left guard pulls, looping behind the center, and blocks the most dangerous man. The center cross-blocks the other defensive tackle. I would have scored easy, and we would have won, 100 percent."

He still carries the photo on his cellphone to remind him of what might have been.

The crushing loss to OU didn't affect Bram's teammates' affection for him, or, for that matter, most observers' assessment of him. His former coach at UH, Kliff Kingsbury, recalls Bram's performance that day with admiration.

"He played his tail off at Oklahoma," Kingsbury says.

"The biggest thing that stuck with me was how much his teammates liked Bram," Kingsbury adds. "He was fun-loving, a leader. People just gravitated towards him."

There was a much bigger challenge waiting in the wings for Bram, though. In five weeks' time, both his teammates' devotion and his coaches' confidence in him would be tested. Bram would face his own worst doubts in the only major college game he would ever start, the final game of his collegiate career.

Chapter 7

Party on the River Walk

IN A STATE KNOWN for its shindigs and fiestas, San Antonio's River Walk is the undisputed Queen of Revelry. Sixth Street in Austin, Dallas' North Greenville Avenue and the newer West Seventh corridor in Fort Worth have their own allure, but they lack the star-spangled romance that lurks around every bend of the San Antonio River as it meanders below street level through downtown.

Along with the restaurants and the luxury hotels that loom over the narrow, serpentine river, with its tropical foliage, its quaint arching footbridges, its colorful lights, its music and its tourist-laden river boats, there are martini bars, margarita bars, wine bars, beer bars, straight-up tequila bars. There are Mexican cantinas, sophisticated hotel lounges and hidden dive bars. There are bars where customers sip and bars where they guzzle. During bowl week, it's more often the latter that fans and football players alike seek out.

As December 2015 wound toward a close in San Antonio, TCU fans drank elbow-to-elbow with visitors from the Pacific Northwest. They crowded into Pat O'Brien's, Jimmy

Buffett's Margaritaville, Howl at the Moon, Durty Nelly's Irish Pub and dozens of other popular hangouts sprinkled along both sides of the winding River Walk.

The Frogs had a highly successful season to celebrate. Toss in New Year's Eve, arriving just two days before the big game, and you had a surefire, 180-proof recipe for a frenetic week-long fiesta.

"It was a great week," says Mark Cohen, TCU's associate athletic director for communications. "It was our first time playing in San Antonio since the '40s, when we played Trinity [University]. We're on the River Walk, we're playing a marquee team in Oregon. There was just a phenomenal buzz.

"We were flying high. We were excited; two highly ranked teams. National media was saying that, of the non-New-Year's-Six games, this was the best game. It was a great week."

As *Fort Worth Star-Telegram* TCU beat writer Carlos Mendez would note in a story leading up to bowl week, playing Pac-12 power Oregon was another milestone in TCU's record of landing in high-profile bowl games against nationally known football programs, including USC in the Rose Bowl in Pasadena, the SEC's Ole Miss in Atlanta's Peach Bowl and Big Ten power Michigan State in Arizona's Buffalo Wild Wings Bowl in Tempe.

The Frogs, especially since joining the Big 12, had stepped up in class: They weren't just playing with the big boys; they'd *become* one of the big boys. Trips to the Weed Whacker Bowls of the world were a distant memory.

"For us, for those kids to get to play on a national stage with bowl games that are nationally relevant, it does wonders for the TCU brand from coast to coast," TCU athletic director Chris Del Conte told Mendez. "The Alamo Bowl in our state is the marquee bowl for recruiting. The date is absolutely perfect in terms of a national audience. For us, recruiting in the state of Texas and being relevant in the state of Texas, the Alamo Bowl is a marquee bowl for us."

Even head coach Gary Patterson, who regularly declared that he approached all bowl games, big or small, with the same win-at-all-costs attitude, was almost effusive in praising the allure of the Alamo Bowl.

"The Alamo Bowl is one of my check-mark bowls," Patterson told Mendez. "I wanted to play in the state, like the Cotton Bowl. You're from Texas, you love all of them when you get a chance to play in front of your home crowd."

• • •

With their bowl date against Oregon locked in, the weary Frogs had had a couple of weeks after their final regular-season game against Baylor to ease through finals and then relax and allow some nagging injuries to heal. Players drifted in for a few voluntary practice sessions.

Soon, though, Patterson and the coaches had summoned everyone back to action with a team meeting in mid-December. For the next two weeks, the Frogs held light practices that gradually grew in tempo and intensity.

"Those first two weeks of practicing are a lot about still getting people healthy," says Bram. "It's kind of like spring practices, looking toward next year. Early on, the coaches gave the two freshmen quarterbacks [Foster Sawyer and Grayson Muehlstein] a lot of snaps to see if either of them might separate themselves.

"Right around the week-and-a-half mark from the game, we start getting game-planned and scripted, putting in plays that will go against the specific looks and defenses we'll be seeing. Trevone was working with the 1s, and I was working with the 2s, sometimes splitting time with the other two guys."

One face was notably absent from the practices, unfortunately: Having suffered a wrist injury against Oklahoma State in the Nov. 7 game, Josh Doctson, the Frogs' All-American receiver, would not be on the field for the Alamo Bowl. He would be sorely missed.

Patterson gave the Frogs Christmas Eve and Christmas Day off. Four days later, they boarded buses and headed south down Interstate 35.

On the bus from Fort Worth to the Alamo City that Monday morning in late December, the Frogs were confident. They'd had a good season that came very close to being great. Under the relentless Patterson, they had a history of success in bowl games. TCU had won seven of its last nine post-season games. The opening line in Vegas had the Frogs listed as favorites by a point and a half.

The first thing Patterson had to do when the team bus arrived in San Antonio was defuse a messy public-relations issue. At the Orange Bowl in Miami, Oklahoma quarterback Baker Mayfield had complained to reporters that Patterson didn't like him and had "hung him out to dry" by reneging on a scholarship offer three years earlier.

Now the sports media awaited the coach's response. Patterson promptly and skillfully downplayed the issue. Yes, the coach confirmed, the Frogs did recruit Mayfield, but they had already been committed to another quarterback and decided they could take only one.

"It was a win-win for everyone, because Baker ended up now being the starter at Oklahoma and we had Trevone Boykin," Patterson told reporters. "To me, both of us won. To me, you just need to get over it."

Then Patterson steered the narrative back to the most important thing on his agenda: beating Oregon on Saturday, just six days away.

"It's like a Baylor, it's like an Oklahoma," Patterson said of facing Oregon and its fourth-ranked offense. "They're a top-10 football team. They're ranked 15th, but they're a team that when their quarterback [Vernon Adams Jr.] has been healthy, just like when we've been healthy, they're hard to deal with. But that's what you want; you want challenges."

He didn't bother to remind reporters that the Frogs' own offense, with the dynamic Boykin at the helm, was ranked third in the country. It had been exactly one month since TCU had closed its 12-game regular season with a 28-21 double-overtime win against Baylor in a driving rainstorm in Fort Worth.

For the players, the party was under way virtually from the time they stepped off their buses. That's what bowl weeks are: one big week-long party for players and fans alike. There are activities and events the players are expected to attend, wrapped around their final practices. But after those, they're on their own.

Players were provided breakfast and lunch at the team hotel — the Hyatt River Walk — and got $30 per day, paid at the beginning of the trip, for dinner and miscellaneous expenses. So the players arrived in San Antonio with a couple of hundred dollars extra rattling around in their pockets. Turned loose in the evenings, they simply walked out the hotel's front door and into the swirling action outside.

The players, of course, were eager to greet friends and classmates driving down from Fort Worth and to let down their hair and have fun on the River Walk. Quarterbacks Trevone Boykin and Bram Kohlhausen were front and center with their TCU teammates in that mission. They'd all earned it, after all.

"Once we arrived in San Antonio, we partied until curfew every night," Bram says. "Going to practice, showing up at bowl events, checking in, then leaving to go drink . . . I honestly thought this was what college athletics, especially bowl trips, was all about."

• • •

Everyone knows now that just two nights before the big game Trevone Boykin would stay too long at the party and wind up sleeping it off in the hoosegow. That he would be suspended and sent back to Fort Worth.

What most people don't know is that, on the same night the Horned Frogs would lose Boykin, they could have lost their No. 2 quarterback as well. Just a couple of hours before Boykin would find himself handcuffed under a pile of San Antonio's finest at 2 in the morning, his buddy Bram had his own confrontation at the very same Pat O'Brien's. Unlike Boykin, Bram — with encouragement from a large and persistent bouncer — had the good sense this time to walk away.

The action went down on Wednesday, a day the players had looked forward to with much anticipation. That was the day the team's cheerleaders and band would arrive, along with many other students coming in for the game. The ongoing celebration was guaranteed to get louder and livelier.

"It was just another excuse to party," Bram confirms. "Wednesday was also our last night with a decent curfew" — midnight, as opposed to 11 p.m. on New Year's Eve. "We were there at Pat O'Brien's, hanging out like we had been all week. It was like a TCU bar that night." The bar was just a half-block from the team hotel, and TCU players had made it their headquarters.

The partying had already run into a snag for Bram and Boykin the night before at Pat O'Brien's, when a bartender had refused to serve Boykin late in the evening, saying Tre had at that point had too much to drink. Sticking up for his teammate, Bram pointed out that he'd been drinking elbow-to-elbow with Boykin all night and that the same bartender had just served *him* two drinks.

This wasn't the first time Bram had stood up for Boykin in a situation where he thought his friend had gotten unequal treatment. A year earlier, on Christmas night during Peach Bowl week, a large contingent of TCU players had begun piling into a bar in Atlanta. A bouncer at the door let everyone else pass but stopped Boykin. The bouncer told Boykin he couldn't enter because he didn't have a belt on and his pants were sagging.

"I pulled off my belt and handed it to Trevone," Bram recalls. "The bouncer said he still couldn't come in. I yelled out, 'OK, everybody, we're leaving.' Thirty guys got up and started heading for the door, and then they said, 'OK, you can stay.' "

On this Tuesday night in San Antonio, though, a bouncer walked over to back up the bartender, and it was Bram and Boykin who ended up bowing out.

"I think I asked, 'How are you going to serve me two and him not even one?' " Bram recalls. "They said he couldn't even walk straight. Then the bouncer told us to leave, and we left."

But they were back the next night, and Pat O'Brien's was rocking, with the newly arriving cheerleaders, band members and other students and fans pouring in.

Bram and one of the cheerleaders, the ex-girlfriend of a teammate, were hanging out, listening to the piano, flirting and talking. Nearby, the ex-boyfriend seethed. Finally, he interrupted the conversation and ordered her to leave the bar. At some point — Bram is vague about the details, saying he doesn't want to embarrass anyone – the cheerleader's drink wound up in her lap.

"At that point, she and I removed ourselves from the situation for half an hour or so," Bram says. "We came back into the bar, got a couple of drinks and we were walking away, heading back outside."

The ex-boyfriend "saw me leaving the bar area with my hands full, two drinks in each hand. He walked up and pushed me with a palm in my face. I hit him once and headed for the exit. A bouncer walked me out and another escorted him [the ex-boyfriend] out. It was around 11:45, time to get back for curfew. Everybody started heading back to the hotel."

Back at the Hyatt, Bram says, "we all made curfew" and were safe in their rooms by the time an assistant coach looked in for the obligatory room check. But Boykin was still thinking about the party that was going on without him out on the River Walk.

"It was just a thought, like, 'Let's go back out,' " Bram says. "We'd talked about that sometimes before, but we never really did it. Nobody would actually pull the trigger. The coaches treat us like big boys. They check that we're in, and then it's on us.

"But that night we got our rooms checked and Trevone wasn't ready to wind down. Preston Miller [a backup running back and wide receiver] said he would go, too. So someone, I don't remember who, said, 'Let's do it,' and [Boykin and Miller] walked out.

"I didn't go back out that night because it was past curfew, and maybe a starter can sneak back out and get away with it. But a backup, if caught, would be made an example of. Besides, I'd already been kicked out of that bar anyway."

Chapter 8

Catastrophe at the 11th Hour

OUT ON THE RIVER WALK, Boykin and Miller hustled back to Pat O'Brien's and continued drinking. Near closing time, a few minutes before 2 a.m., Boykin found himself the target of heckling by some fans, presumably Oregon supporters, who had recognized him. Fueled by alcohol, Boykin reacted violently.

The club's bouncers stepped in as the fight spread to the sidewalk outside. Miller and a group of TCU fans intervened, finally separating Boykin from the scrum and pushing him toward the hotel, just as police were arriving. For a moment, it appeared the night — and Boykin — might be saved. But TCU would not be so lucky twice in a row.

Enraged by something one of the bouncers said, Boykin broke away from Miller and the TCU fans and charged back into the fray, but now it was the cops who were involved. Trevone was swinging "indiscriminately," according to the police report, and connected with one of the officers.

According to San Antonio Police Chief William McManus' statement later to reporters, Boykin had struck a bicycle officer in the face. TCU's star quarterback was taken to the ground, and officers threatened to tase him if he didn't stop resisting. Handcuffs went on, and Boykin was ushered to jail.

"We don't know whether he was swinging at the officer or whether he was swinging at somebody behind" the officer, McManus told reporters later. "I don't know, but in any event, the officer was struck in the face." The officer, McManus said, suffered bruises, an abrasion and a swollen face.

Back at the hotel, Bram's cellphone began to buzz. Even as the police officers were getting Boykin subdued and handcuffed, Miller was frantically calling Bram.

"I was literally talking to [Miller] while Trevone still had the cops on top of him. I guess I wasn't completely shocked, because of Trevone's demeanor and behavior at that time, and not just him." After the Oklahoma State loss, Bram explained, "it kind of became an angry season for all of us. If people talked smack to us, we talked back. Then you add alcohol . . ."

If Bram wasn't entirely blindsided, the same couldn't be said for the Purple Nation of TCU fans. TCU's star quarterback, at one point the Heisman Trophy front-runner and the heart of the Frogs' offense, behind bars? Holy heart attack, Batman!

How would Coach Patterson — a man who fervently lived his life by a certain code of conduct and expected the same from his players — react? A suspension seemed inevitable. How could the Frogs possibly beat Oregon, already a tough proposition, without Boykin running the show?

For TCU athletics officials, there were no optimistic answers to the barrage of questions that would be forthcoming from both the media and the fans. This was a bona fide purple nightmare.

"I get that phone call about 4 in the morning," says Frogs communications honcho Mark Cohen. "Of course, I'm asleep.

The phone rings. I see the 210 area code, and I just thought, 'Whatever.' I let it go to voice mail. But I couldn't go back to sleep. A couple of minutes later I see that somebody had left a message. I figure telemarketer or something, but I listen to the voicemail, and it's a radio station in San Antonio and this voice said, 'We want to confirm that Trevone Boykin has been arrested.'

"I'm like, 'No! No! No!' But I did what you do nowadays; I checked Twitter and I see a couple of reports coming in. About that time, I get another call, and it's a TV station in San Antonio wanting to see if we had a statement about Trevone Boykin's arrest."

Cohen's first move was to alert Chris Del Conte, who was TCU's athletic director. Boykin, as it turned out, was being charged with assault on a public servant, a third-degree felony, as well as public intoxication and resisting arrest.

The first issue for Del Conte and Coach Patterson was to deal with what came next for Boykin. They would have to arrange bail and then render the appropriate discipline, no matter how painful it might be. There was no hesitation and little discussion. Both men knew what had to be done. Boykin and Miller would be suspended and sent directly home.

Meanwhile, Del Conte and Cohen began the process of devising a plan to deal with news that obviously would not reflect well on TCU.

"I speak to strategic-communications and public-relations classes here on campus all the time," Cohen says, "and I always talk about the joys of the job, the relationships with student athletes, watching them celebrate after a win. That's the best part of the job. But sometimes a student will ask me what's the worst part, or the least favorite memory you have, and I'll say, it's that Alamo Bowl experience and what happened with Trevone.

"He was so beloved, I mean, as popular as can be. I remember at 'Meet the Frogs' that year -- it's always the Saturday before the season opener, from 1 to 3 p.m. — and here's Trevone Boykin, a Heisman Trophy candidate, staying till 5 o'clock that day, two hours later than he was supposed to, because the line of fans for him was just out the door. He felt like, 'I can't leave with all these people wanting my autograph.'

"Trevone was a guy who was at the height of popularity with TCU fans. I remember that morning, it was all over the news; it was the top story on *Sports Center*, it was the No. 1 trending story. To just see it come down to, 'Wow, this is how it's going to end for him . . .'"

TCU offensive coordinator Doug Meacham will remember that night for the rest of his life, too.

"It was late, sometime early in the morning, you get that phone call, first one around 2. Then at 5 a.m., Tre calls. From that point on, your night is done. There will be no sleep.

"What are we gonna do? What's our next move? There's no preparation for it, just sadness for Tre and our players. But it opened the door for Bram to do what he did.

"There was never a discussion about how we could maneuver through this thing and let Tre play. It was, 'Hey, he made his choice, and now he's got to go home.' "

It was Meacham who was the first coach to make a call to Bram, around 4 a.m. He told the Frogs' No. 2 quarterback to get ready to play. Bram says he hadn't even thought about the game; he was more concerned about his friend, Trevone.

In fact, Bram had already called home, right after the call from Miller outside Pat O'Brien's, seeking help from his mom in finding his friend.

"I get a phone call from Bram in the middle of the night, early Thursday morning," says Donna Kohlhausen. "I was home in bed; we were going up [to San Antonio] on New

Year's Day. Bram said, 'Mom, you've got to help me find Trevone. He's been arrested.' I said, 'What in the world are you talking about?' "

Rubbing sleep from her eyes, Donna Kohlhausen had begun a computer search, hoping to ferret out exactly where Boykin was being held. She had followed up with phone calls to various police numbers. Somcone finally confirmed that Trevone was in the San Antonio jail and wouldn't be out before late in the morning.

The next team official to call Bram was Cumbie, the co-offensive coordinator and quarterbacks coach. It was still hours before dawn. Shortly after that, quality control coach Jake Brown slipped a game script under Bram's hotel room door. The now-starting quarterback in the Valero Alamo Bowl had lost his original copy.

Back in Houston, Donna Kohlhausen fired off texts to her other two sons, alerting them that Bram was going to start Saturday against Oregon. Dash and Gareth found that difficult to comprehend.

"They said, 'Oh, Mom, what are you talking about?' It got pretty exciting around here. Patterson wasn't saying, but Bram had been told, so we knew."

"I would sometimes joke with Trevone, 'Look, I don't want you to get badly hurt, but Bram needs a little more playing time,' Donna says.

"I told him after the bowl game, 'I didn't want you to go this far.' "

• • •

The TCU players who hadn't gotten a call or text during the night began waking up to the shattering news Thursday morning. New Year's Eve, the last day of 2015, was suddenly becoming the worst day of the year for the Horned Frogs. No Boykin against the Ducks? The news was a gut punch for some, a grit-your-teeth-and-get-tougher moment for others, a painfully complicated combination of those reactions for the rest.

A few of Boykin's teammates, including senior guard Bobby Thompson, had warned him about breaking curfew and sidestepped the temptation to do so themselves. Still, they had never expected to wake up to the news that Boykin had been arrested and suspended.

"We were all together the night before," recalls Thompson, who was the roommate of sophomore tight end Charlie Reid. "We told Tre, 'Hey, man, that's not a good idea.' He said, 'Well, I'm going by myself then. We told him we weren't going with him.

"At 4 in the morning, I'm in the room with Charlie Reid and I hear a knock on the door. I asked Charlie if he heard it, too. He said, 'Yeah, someone's at the door.' So I go and look out the peephole in the door and there's Coach Patterson, Coach Cumbie, Chris Del Conte and some other guys.

"I turned and asked Charlie, 'Are we in trouble?' Finally, I open the door and they walk in and turn the light on. Someone says, 'Where is he?' and I realize they're looking for Tre. We told them we'd tried to talk him out of going. After they left, we still didn't know what had actually happened. Two hours later I'm getting texts from people asking, 'What happened? What happened?' "

They wouldn't know for sure for a few more hours, Charlie Reid recalls.

"It was 6 or 7 the next morning, and I woke up with big Bob shaking me over and over again. He said Trevone had been arrested."

When they finally heard Boykin had been arrested, Reid says, "we knew that meant he'd be going home. Here we were at the Alamo Bowl, having a great time, and the wind was taken out of our sails. We were confident, but we were bummed out, let down. We hated it for Trevone, who was a phenomenal player.

"It wasn't about Bram or a lack of confidence in him, but Trevone had been the heart of our offense and our team. It was a tough loss, a big hit. You look to the next guy. You give him your full support. You let him know you trust him, that you're behind him. I think Bram knew that everyone had faith in him."

As for Bram, the game wasn't the first thing on his mind when he heard about the arrest.

"Immediately, I wasn't thinking about football. I just wanted Trevone out of jail as quickly as possible.

"He came back to the hotel to pack his things, and I was his roommate, so I texted the other quarterbacks that he was here and to come see him, give him a big hug and just give him some sort of support.

"This guy was in the Heisman conversation all season, then he makes a mistake and cannot play in the last game of his senior year. I know it eats at him to this day.

"I felt really bad for him," Bram says. "He was a captain; he let us down and he knew it. All we could do was give him encouraging words. When it was just me and him, we talked about what happened. Then, when more people started coming in, it was just him packing and guys giving him hugs, and coaches talking about rebounding and stuff. It was really awkward.

"He never apologized or anything at the time, but you could tell he was just in a whirlwind of emotion. He'd just been arrested, probably didn't sleep well, and now he was packing his things. I kind of know what it feels like, because I made a mistake and couldn't play in my final high school game because of a broken hand. I still regret that decision."

• • •

Meanwhile, the news had been racing through the Frogs' entire traveling party like an electric shock wave. Longtime TCU play-by-play radio broadcaster Brian Estridge couldn't believe what he was hearing.

"It was kind of a range of emotions. I was looking forward to seeing how this team stacked up against a program like Oregon's . . . I was really anticipating the game. We had a good senior class talent-wise. It was going to be a terrific challenge, really a benchmark game for the program. Oregon had been really good for the last several years, and TCU was trying to be an elite program.

"Then Trevone happened, and all those emotions shifted. It was 'Oh, my word, what's this going to be like?' I was obviously concerned about how the Frogs would react, mentally and emotionally.

"I was disappointed. I was disappointed in Trevone and for Trevone. But I was also disappointed for that team, because of all the excitement going in. They wouldn't be playing fully loaded. I thought it was a very selfish move by Trevone and one that would affect him for the rest of his life. And I think it's safe to say that it has," Estridge says.

"But they are just kids, and they don't realize the impact something like this could have on the rest of their lives. When Trevone Boykin walked into that bar, he wasn't thinking about the NFL draft, or some day in the future when he might be sitting across a desk from a TCU alum during a job interview. He was just thinking about that bucket of beer."

Gil LeBreton, then a sports columnist for the *Fort Worth Star-Telegram,* got the word early on New Year's Eve morning: "Right away everyone was saying, 'Boykin? No way!' We just assumed that there was no way TCU was going to win the football game without its star quarterback. There was a lot of lamenting and hand-wringing for the Frogs after that."

The morning after his arrest, Boykin faced an appearance at the city magistrate's office at 10:30 Thursday. After a $5,000 bond was posted, he eventually walked out with his jacket pulled over his head, shielding himself from the cameras as he got into the passenger seat of a silver SUV driven by a university employee.

Boykin did not comment to reporters but later posted a public apology on Twitter:

"I truly let down my family, teammates and the TCU and Fort Worth communities who have supported me so much. I have no excuses for my very poor decision, and I'm embarrassed about it. My teammates are my brothers. There's nothing I wanted to do more than play one last game with my fellow seniors."

Coach Patterson's own statement that morning brought home the stark reality to TCU fans: "Trevone Boykin and Preston Miller have been suspended for Saturday's game due to a violation of team rules. We are disappointed in their actions and apologize to the TCU Horned Frogs Nation, the Valero Alamo Bowl and city of San Antonio."

• • •

As fate would have it, both the bowl teams were scheduled to attend a news conference Thursday morning. Naturally, the Boykin news dominated TCU's portion of it.

"I remember the morning that happened with Trevone — unfortunate timing — it was offensive media day," recalls Frogs communications director Cohen. "So we're having to go to a press conference with the two [offensive] coordinators, and we had three or four players available. Obviously, Bram wasn't one of them.

"I'll never forget this – Doug Meacham blanked out on Bram's name at the podium. You know, there's a little pressure when you have all the cameras on you, and I think somebody asked, 'Who's going to start?' Doug was the lead OC, and he said, 'We're going to go with, uh, um . . .' And I think Sonny kind of whispered Bram's name, and Doug said, 'Yeah, Bram Kohlhausen.' "

Patterson, for his part, told reporters he'd had no choice but to suspend the two players who broke curfew. The decision was especially agonizing, he acknowledged, because it involved the team's star player, someone who was so essential to the psyche of the team.

"It's unfortunate for him, because Trevone has meant so much to TCU," the coach told the assembled media. "We love him, but he understands. Obviously, as head coaches, you have to make decisions, do things sometimes you don't want to do.

"You're not just teaching *him*, you're teaching the other 120 guys that are on your team, that they understand that all your actions have a reaction, and you have to learn from it. Let's just say that nothing [unlawful] happened, but he's bragging that he jumped curfew and he went out and played a great game. Then I'm going to have the same problem next year. One of the things I think people don't give head coaches enough credit for is trying to raise men," he reminded the reporters.

Unhappy that he couldn't control the media narrative — ESPN's *Sports Center* was leading with the story every hour and fans across the country were buzzing about Boykin's suspension — Patterson wanted to shift the focus from Boykin's arrest to the upcoming game and his players who would be performing in it. So he lit into the assembled reporters.

"Let me say this to you: I was a little disappointed that everything that was basically talked to my kids about [by reporters] was about Trevone Boykin. We're here to play Oregon. If we're going to make this a press conference about him, then I think we're ruining San Antonio and the bowl game and we're saying that everybody else that plays at TCU is not important," Patterson admonished the press corps.

"Really, my feelings went out to him [Boykin] and for my team, because, obviously, he's the starter," Patterson continued. "He's a veteran, but we'll play another quarterback, and they'll do just fine.

"Just like anybody else, I'm a fan. I want to see Vernon [Adams Jr., the Ducks' starting QB] vs. Trevone. You want to see it all. You came here, got to the end of the year, you want that last ballgame to be everything you want.

"Hopefully, it is."

Running back Aaron Green, a San Antonio native, was one of a handful of offensive players TCU sent to the press conference. He voiced what many TCU players felt about Boykin.

"I'm hurting from it," Green said. "I'm not going to sit up here and lie. He's a kid with an extremely bright future, probably one of the best football players I've ever played with. He's a good person, too. So, I mean, you just hate to see that happen, you know?

"You just got to make good decisions, know when to be in your room, not break curfew. And remember, we're here to play a football game above all things."

With the Vegas line having lurched from TCU by 1 to Oregon favored by 8, both Green and TCU receiver Kolby Listenbee insisted to reporters that they actually relished being the underdog.

"I love when people count us out," Green said. "I feel like that's when I play my best ball. Go ahead, count me out."

Added Listenbee, "I feel like we're all about shocking the world, really."

He had no idea how prophetic his words would be.

• • •

As the Frogs gathered for that afternoon's practice, their first without Boykin, a few players lamented out loud their chances of defeating Oregon without their star. Bram Kohlhausen heard them, but he also heard those who made it a point to slap him on the back, telling him he could do it, wishing him luck.

"After Trevone left the team, we just had to go back to business," Bram recalls. "We had practice later that day, and, as harsh as it sounds, it was next man up. That was me. It was very nerve-wracking.

"I could definitely hear the 'we are f*cked' voices. I just had to block those out. But I could definitely also hear the 'Bram's got this' voices.

"Coach Cumbie has every quarterback on the roster fully prepared for every game. He does this thing called 'reps in the back' where all quarterbacks that are not running the plays at that point go through the steps for each play that the quarterback that is in is running. I knew the plays. I had studied the playbook intensely. I even had my girlfriend at the time quiz me on every play in the script.

"I practiced with the [first team] on Thursday morning, then again during our walk-through Friday."

Tight end Charlie Reid confirms that Bram was ready: "Through the bowl practices, you run the same plays for two or three weeks. We had the game plan ingrained in our heads. Bram was prepared. Physically and mentally, he was ready to rock and roll.

"Give credit to Sonny Cumbie. He gets those quarterbacks right. Sitting in on his meetings now as a graduate assistant, he's so thorough. He would have had anybody ready."

It wasn't as if the Frogs hadn't played without Boykin

before. They'd beaten Kansas after Trevone was injured early in that game; then Bram had rallied them against Oklahoma before their eventual 30-29 loss.

But this wasn't Kansas the Frogs would be lining up to play without Boykin Saturday evening. This was 15th-ranked Oregon, a team riding a six-game winning streak; a team that had scored 38 points or more in nine of its 12 games and on four occasions had put up more than 50.

Bram didn't have to worry about the Ducks' offense, of course; that job would fall to Patterson's vaunted defense. Bram just had to find a way to put points on the board.

The biggest problem for Bram to overcome had nothing to do with his playing ability or readiness. The challenge was gaining control of the emotional roller coaster he'd been riding all season. There'd been his dad's long illness and eventual passing, less than two months before. Now he'd had to say goodbye to his roommate, one of his best friends on the team, who was leaving in disgrace. It was almost as if someone else close to Bram had died.

The shock was real for the rest of the TCU team, too. It seemed as if Boykin's haymaker hadn't just hit a police officer but had caught his TCU teammates square on the chin as well. They were dazed, confused, in shock. Could they shake it off in just 48 hours?

For most of the team, the place they went to try was back to the River Walk bars for New Year's Eve that night.

"That Thursday night after walk-through, I had more than a few margaritas," Bram says. "Maybe it was because I was scared, or nervous, but who knows?"

Chapter 9
Game Day

BRAM HAD BARELY pried his eyes open on the morning of Jan. 2, 2016, when he felt the difference in his room at the Hyatt Regency River Walk. It felt empty. Silent. There was no sound from the TV, where ESPN's SportsCenter would normally already be playing on game day. No sense of someone shuffling around, getting dressed on the other side of the room. No splashing of a shower running in the bathroom. Nothing.

Trevone isn't here, Bram remembered.

No roommate sharing a joke about the evening's upcoming game. No one to laugh with about their revelries on the River Walk that week. No Trevone Boykin, Heisman Trophy candidate, to lean on, to believe in, to lead the Frogs to victory over the formidable Ducks.

No Trevone. Just me.

"Typically Trevone would wake up first and watch whatever was on SportsCenter," Bram says. "He was usually amped for the game, so he was always up early.

"It was really, really weird not having him in the room. The entire vibe was just different. We had roomed on the road together all season. Usually, I would wake up to Trevone in the shower, playing his favorite songs, turned up loud. Then he would leave and go down for breakfast and I would go through my routine.

"My routine was typically a lot slower than Trevone's. I would sit up in bed, scroll through my phone, watch SportsCenter, then shower and head down. This was a night game, so everything is just a little slower. Breakfast was longer. Meetings were later. Then we just hang out until we're ready to have a pre-game meal and go to the stadium."

After hoisting River Walk margaritas Thursday night, Bram and his teammates had hustled back to the hotel for an 11 o'clock curfew. At midnight, the entire team had gathered in a conference room for a brief team meeting, and together players and staff had toasted the new year, 2016, with sparkling hard cider.

If anyone noted the irony, after the amount of booze that had already been consumed during the week, it went unspoken.

The gathering was meant to be a bonding moment. Without Boykin, though, the good cheer was clearly forced. An air of affected bravado permeated the room. Boykin's absence left a hole at the heart of the team.

The next day, Friday, Bram and other players had drifted into the training room, sitting for routine intravenous hydration. After a team dinner, meetings started at 8 p.m. Lights out was two hours later, at 10. The week-long cursed fiesta had finally ground to a halt.

Bram's wake-up call Saturday morning came at 8:30, along with the realization that he was about to play the last game of his college career and would be the starting quarterback for the first time.

No Trevone, the empty room whispered again.

After showering, he pulled on shorts and a T-shirt, slipped on his shower shoes and went downstairs. As always on game day, he had a light breakfast, some scrambled eggs and fruit.

"We usually had a quarterbacks position meeting around 9:30. This is when we get our QB 'homework' back from Cumbie that we'd turned in the night before. This was us drawing up all the plays on the script and verbalizing our reads on paper. Cumbie would correct or add to anything that was not included.

"Then we'd have a legit casual walk-through where people are in slip-ons or sandals in one of the hotel meeting rooms. After that, we are basically instructed to get off our feet and relax until we had a lunch buffet from like noon to 2. After lunch is when people started to get treatment on existing injuries or get IVs before the game."

As he had on Friday, Bram showed up in the training room for an IV, hoping to wash the week-long fun out of his system. He still couldn't get Trevone off his mind, but he knew his focus now had to be on the game.

"After he left the morning he got bailed out, we had exchanged a few text messages," Bram recalls of Trevone. "But at that point I had to be a little selfish and make sure I was prepared. I was worried more about how I was going to handle this game.

"I believe he wished me luck before the game, but he was upset he had let everyone down, so he was handling his own stuff. I think he and his mom watched the game at his uncle's house in South Dallas and played dominoes."

Back in his room after lunch, Bram tried to study his game script while fielding a flood of texts from family and friends. Many were just arriving in San Antonio after learning that he would be starting against Oregon.

"A family group chat was in full effect as they did some pre-game tailgating at the Tower of the Americas," Bram said. "One specific conversation I had was with James Power, my roommate and long snapper on the 2014 team. He was really good at keeping my mind off of everything. He asked me what my celebration was going to be after I scored. I told him I was going to 'stir it up' like James Harden, who is my favorite basketball player."

Then, two hours before the 5:45 p.m. kickoff, it was time to board the buses to the stadium.

As the players entered the locker room, they were reminded again of who wasn't there. Boykin's locker was the first one on the left, right beside Bram's. Its emptiness was like a silent scream in the crowded room.

While players individually drifted out to the field to stretch and loosen up, adjusting to the lighting and surroundings of the Alamodome, Bram's nerves made it hard for him to sit still. He made his way to the training room to get his ankles taped. He reviewed Cumbie's game script again, listening to music through his headphones. Sixty minutes before kickoff, the Frogs returned to the field as a team.

The quarterbacks each put in some individual work, then gathered for a pat-and-go drill with the wide receivers. As always, the first-team offense came together to run a couple of plays. Then, 20 minutes before kickoff, the Frogs retreated to the locker room for final preparations.

"At this point I was confident in our game plan. I tried to give off a calm vibe," Bram says. "I had just come off the Oklahoma game, so I was walking around with a lot of confidence. I knew everyone remembered that we scored a lot of points in Norman when I was in the game.

"I was worried about how the other players were going to come out. Some came out flat, but as the game went on, the younger guys who were getting a chance to play because of injuries were ready to go."

The game plan, of course, had been "set up to fit Trevone," Coach Meacham recalls, "with a quarterback run game and plays that suited his athletic style. Instead of changing the whole game plan, we had tried to chisel it down to what we thought Bram could do within that game plan that we'd practiced for three weeks. It was watered down. We wanted to see what would happen, could he get it done, was he hot, was he not?"

• • •

Oregon won the coin toss, and almost before Bram knew it, TCU was kicking off and the game was under way. Good kickoff coverage and a second-down sack of quarterback Vernon Adams Jr. by defensive end Josh Carraway forced Oregon into a three-and-out on its first possession, setting the stage for Bram.

Bram was up, with excellent early field position. But his under-pressure third-down pass ticked off Kolby Listenbee's outstretched fingers.

A completion would have put the Frogs in business, deep in Ducks territory. Instead, the Ducks took the ensuing punt and marched down the field, gashing the Frogs with several up-the-middle runs before Adams torched safety Derrick Kindred with a 37-yard touchdown pass to a wide-open Darren Carrington as he crossed into the end zone. It was the beginning of an Oregon mudslide that would bury the Frogs by halftime.

"Realistically, on our first possession we should have scored on our third-down play," recalls Bram, "but it went right off Listenbee's hands.

"The whole first half was a combination of things going wrong. The defense would get them in third-and-long and then they would hit a long play. Our secondary was awful.

"They were throwing up prayers and coming down with every single catch.

"What upset me the most offensively was that we would keep getting dumb penalties. There were probably four or five big penalties — holding, personal fouls — that kept putting us in the hole."

Tight end Charlie Reid echoes Bram's assessment: "Everything that could go wrong did go wrong. We just played sloppy football. It just felt like everything was going their way and nothing was going right for us."

Bram's state of mind was worsening with each play.

"It got to the point before halftime where I was becoming predictable because I was so frustrated," he says. "I threw a really bad interception into their two-high coverage. That was the most upsetting play for me because I thought that terrible read was justification enough to bench me."

The frustration was also being felt by TCU officials in the press box and by the hordes of purple-clad fans who had made the Alamo Bowl look like a Frogs home game.

Among those in the press box was Frogs communications chief Mark Cohen, who recalls: "That first half, we just couldn't stop them. Bram didn't play horribly, but it was just mistakes. We'd get a couple first downs, then get a penalty."

"What summed up the first half: We blocked a punt and they recovered and got a first down. You're like, this is just not our day. And the guy who recovered the punt was a walk-on who wasn't even on the team the next year."

By the end of the first quarter, Oregon had bulldozed to a 21-0 lead. TCU, on the other hand, had managed just two first downs.

It would get worse. On the Ducks' first possession of

the second quarter, Tony Brooks-James slashed through the Frogs' defense for 47 yards to set up his own five-yard touchdown run.

TCU's defense was in tatters, but Kohlhausen and the Frogs' offense hadn't been any better. By halftime the Frogs had rushed for just 46 yards. Bram had completed just nine of 19 passes for 96 yards, and the team had totaled an embarrassing five first downs.

"Their quarterback was going up and down on the field on us," Coach Meacham recalls. "We'd drive, stutter, move it, but not enough to punch in and score."

TCU's highlight moment in the first half, in fact, was forcing the Ducks to settle for a 47-yard field goal with 32 seconds left before intermission, to give the Ducks a final first-half tally of 31 points.

And not once during that first half did anyone hear the deep-throated blare of TCU's famous train horn, the one that rocks Amon Carter Stadium whenever the Frogs score. In the noise and clamor of the Alamodome, it sat as silent witness to the Frogs' humiliation. No one had expected Patterson's always competitive defense to get completely steamrolled.

"Honestly," says Bram, "I think going into the game, just keeping the game close was my goal.

"Thirty-one-zip was horrible. Going into the game I knew we could keep it close; maybe a few things would go our way and we could score some points. But I never imagined being down 31-0. We just got our asses handed to us."

• • •

In the stands with the Kohlhausen clan, family friend Susan Hunt was finding the debacle too painful to watch.

"It was so awful you just wanted to close your eyes the whole time and just listen. At halftime, it was brutal. I didn't think they'd put him back in, and I thought I would leave. I didn't want to jinx him any longer. I went outside the stadium in the rain and just stood there."

Back inside the stadium, thousands of TCU fans were feeling their own misery. Even Dick Lowe, arguably TCU's No. 1 fan, found himself wishing he were someplace else. The Fort Worth oilman, a top benefactor of the Frogs' football program, had flown down the day before the game with family and friends, still upset by the Boykin news. Watching the Frogs fall apart in the first half hadn't helped his disposition one bit:

"I'd have left at the half, but we came in a charter bus, and it wasn't supposed to pick us up until after the game," Lowe recalled in an interview before his death in late 2020. "I was shocked that they were that much better than us. That surprised the heck out of me."

In the press box, the writers for the Frogs' hometown *Star-Telegram* were stunned by the carnage too.

TCU beat writer Carlos Mendez knew the Frogs had been shell-shocked by the Boykin suspension, but an Oregon blowout of this proportion was the last thing he'd expected.

Trying to understand the debacle, he figured that "you really can't ask any team to recover from losing a player like [Boykin]. It wasn't like they lost their No. 1 running back; they lost their Heisman Trophy candidate quarterback.

"Teams feed off their quarterback. Kohlhausen wasn't playing terrible, but he wasn't effective either. This wasn't a team that was charged up and on its mental game. It was a team that was still reeling from what had happened," Mendez says.

"The way the game rolled out," says TCU play-by-play man Estridge, "you had to be thinking, 'Bram's overmatched.' You had the Trevone story, the emotion that Bram was going through about that. You couldn't lose sight of the fact that this was a 20-year-old kid going through this."

For columnist LeBreton's part, "I thought the big difference in the first half was at quarterback. Oregon had Vernon Adams, and he was one of the most underrated really good quarterbacks in the country. TCU had a great defense, and they couldn't stop him.

"I thought the Frogs were playing with a hangover from losing Boykin during the week. They were also without Josh Doctson, their best receiver.

"We didn't know anything about Bram. He'd played well at Oklahoma, and I knew he was capable, but when his own defense spots them a 31-point lead . . . I've been doing this a long time, and I'd never seen a team come back from 31 points down," LeBreton says.

From Coach Cumbie's perch in the press box, he couldn't think of any game comparable to the debacle that had just unfolded either.

"We were pretty pitiful in the first half. I was in the press box thinking that since I'd been at TCU we'd never been beaten like this. You come in at halftime and there are no words," Cumbie recalls.

"When the Frogs fell behind 31-0," LeBreton says, "my column was writing itself. My lede [newspaper jargon for the opening paragraph] was going to be something about how badly things had been going for them all week. There was the Boykin suspension, and it had rained, Oregon weather. It just wasn't the Frogs' week.

"For once in my career, I was pretty well finished by the time halftime was coming to an end," LeBreton recalls.

"I don't usually like having three-fourths of my column done at halftime. That's an invitation for some sort of black magic to happen."

• • •

Black magic — or, in TCU's case, perhaps, purple magic — was indeed brewing, though few realized it as they contemplated the first-half bloodbath.

Near the end of the first quarter, Oregon center Matt Hegarty had limped off the field with an injury that would sideline him for the rest of the game. In the second quarter, Hegarty's replacement, Doug Brenner, had struggled with his snaps back to Vernon Adams.

Then, late in the second quarter, Adams had faked an inside handoff and tried to turn up field on the left side with no protection. He was met head on by fast-closing safety Derrick Kindred. The impact of the collision reverberated in the stands.

"We knew when Kindred hit him, he was out," recalls TCU tight end Reid.

"Adams keeps it and takes a huge hit . . . my goodness!" play-by-play announcer Adam Amin exclaimed on ESPN's national broadcast. "And we'll hope that Adams is OK . . . I don't think he is. Now that would definitely change this game."

Adams lay crumpled on the field as Oregon trainers rushed out to tend to their injured player. The Ducks' talented quarterback was barely moving an arm, trying to lift his head.

Just moments earlier, Amin's partner, color analyst Mack Brown, had commented on TCU coach Patterson's animated sideline behavior after the Frogs had foiled Oregon's pass attempt on a fake punt:

"I told you, now, Gary Patterson is going to compete, and these kids are not going to quit, so don't turn this game off, folks. We still got a chance to have a great game here at the end."

Did Brown really believe that, or was he just trying to hold onto an audience that was already reaching for the remote? Either way, now a shaken Adams, the biggest difference-maker in the game to that point, was being escorted to the Oregon locker room. His return seemed highly unlikely.

All three of Oregon's regular-season losses had come when Adams was out with a finger injury. This time, though, the Ducks held a huge lead. Backup quarterback Jeff Lockie had stepped in to lead them to that field goal right before halftime. And back in South Dallas, Trevone Boykin, the player who would have made the biggest difference for TCU, was playing dominoes instead of quarterback.

But the tenor of the game had clearly changed with Adams' departure. TCU didn't have its starting quarterback, and now Oregon didn't either. It was Kohlhausen vs. Lockie, backup vs. backup.

Recalls Bram's high-school teammate Zach Mafrige, who was in the stands for the game: "Knowing their backup didn't have the experience of their starter, we knew that could be a break for the Frogs. The backup wasn't ready to be in that situation. We knew it was now backup vs. backup and that Bram had the edge there."

Under most circumstances, TCU would have been more than happy with that scenario. Trailing 31-0, however, was not one of those circumstances. The biggest question remained: Would Bram even be given a chance to match up with Lockie after such a dismal first-half performance?

Almost before the Frogs could return to their locker room to regroup, ESPN was informing its viewing audience that Oregon's mathematical odds of winning the 2016 Alamo Bowl now stood at 99.1 percent. That left TCU's statistical chance of winning at 0.9 percent.

For most of those watching, that number also pretty much summed up the chances of Bram Kohlhausen's still playing quarterback for TCU when the second half started.

Chapter 10

Halftime Blues

THE DISCUSSION at halftime among the Kohlhausen clan and their friends wasn't about whether TCU had any chance of coming back from a 31-0 deficit. It centered on whether to stay for the next quarter or adjourn to the bar.

Bram's brother Gareth, for one, had seen enough. Watching Oregon dismantle Gary Patterson's fabled defense and his brother Bram struggle to spark the Frogs' offense had been almost more than he could bear.

Gareth loved his brother; he'd come to love TCU football, too. The prospect of watching the Oregon Ducks continue their frolic over the Frogs while Bram sat in disgrace on the bench wasn't something he believed he could stomach.

His fiancé and his older brother Dash took the other side of the argument, and they talked Gareth into having another beer while Dash tried to persuade his brother to stick it out for Bram's sake.

"Basically, we knew the Frogs would have to score every possession to get back into it," Gareth recalls. "Dash said, 'OK, the first possession they don't score, I'll let you leave.'

And if they didn't start Bram in the second half, we were all going to leave. At one point in the second half, we even said, if they have to kick another field goal, we'll head to the bar.

"One turnover, one Oregon touchdown, one fumble, one interception . . . it changes everything, and we're out of there. It wasn't like we were rooting for it, but it was definitely in the back of our minds. I don't know if we would have actually left, but I sure wasn't happy."

Bram's friend Luke Schreiner, on the other hand, was firmly in the "stay" camp. He'd been close with Bram since rooming with some of Bram's high school buddies at UT, and he had joined the Kohlhausen contingent at the game in support of his buddy.

"It gets to halftime and it's 31-0," says Schreiner, "and my buddies are looking at me asking, 'Should we leave?' I told them, 'I can't leave.' I was supposed to meet up with Bram after the game.

"Dash wasn't even thinking Bram would start the second half, with how Coach Patterson is, being superstitious. We even put $20 bets on it. I said Bram would start; Dash said he wouldn't. I figured I was there for Bram and wouldn't be there otherwise. It wasn't Bram's fault, really. The defense gave up all the points."

The same kind of debate was going on among other friends and fans of Bram, there in the Alamodome and elsewhere in front of TV sets.

Watching in Los Angeles, L.A. Harbor coach Reuben Ale had been thrilled and excited to see his former quarterback starting the Alamo Bowl.

By halftime, though, he was reaching for the antacid tablets.

"Oh, my gosh. My eyes were glued on that game. I watched it from start to finish. I was pulling so hard for Bram.

Unfortunately, Boykin had that situation, and I thought, 'Hey, Bram's going to get his shot tonight.' "

After those disastrous first two quarters, though, Ale wasn't expecting to see Bram back on the field for the second half: "I figured that they would want to get the game in the books and get some momentum for next year with a younger quarterback."

In the Alamodome stands, Bram's high-school buddies Zach Mafrige and Nick Kaldis weren't betting on seeing Bram on the field in the second half either, despite their loyalty to him.

"When I heard Bram was starting that game, I had tickets within 15 minutes. I'd followed his career throughout. I knew how hard he'd worked," said former teammate Mafrige.

"I recall very well that if Bram hadn't walked out to start the second half, we wouldn't have stuck it out. I was thinking these guys are getting their ass kicked and Oregon was going to be handed the trophy at the end. But I wouldn't have been there to see it."

There was one person in Bram's crew, though, who knew she wasn't going anywhere no matter what happened in the game's second half, and that was Donna Kohlhausen:

"They were talking about leaving. I said I couldn't, I have to be here; Bram will need somebody's shoulder to cry on. I was absolutely convinced Bram wasn't coming out of that locker room. I don't know who made that stupid decision to leave him in, but they must be patting themselves on the back now."

• • •

Given the option, Bram might have gladly packed up and left for the bar, too. Instead, he kept waiting for one of the coaches to tell him that redshirt freshman Foster Sawyer would be taking over at quarterback.

The embarrassment Bram was feeling extended throughout TCU's locker room. This wasn't TCU football. This wasn't the team that had come within a missed 2-point conversion pass of upsetting Oklahoma and winning the Big 12. This wasn't representative of the program that Gary Patterson had built over 15 seasons of excellence.

With the way the Frogs had come apart in the first half, it was fair to wonder what form the fallout might take in the locker room. Would Patterson simply explode? Would he rant and rave? Would he bench the whole first team? Anything seemed possible. The only completely ludicrous scenario was that TCU could somehow come back and win the game.

But Gary Patterson had never quit on a game at halftime, and he wasn't going to start on Jan. 2, 2016, no matter what the score might be.

"When I went in at halftime," says Frogs communications director Cohen, "I didn't hear anyone ranting. I've seen unpleasant locker rooms. I've seen Gary upset, but this was actually calm.

"Gary is good at recognizing what players need. He knows when to lay low and when to come on hard."

The most outwardly emotional move the head coach made at halftime was yanking off his sweat-drenched shirt — a black knit polo with university logo — and pulling on a fresh short-sleeved polo in emphatic TCU purple.

"As usual, there's part of a game [when] as a head coach you're not very smart," Patterson was to tell *The Dallas Morning News'* Chuck Carlton when TCU returned to the Alamo Bowl three years later. "That's why I changed shirts, to become smarter with the color."

What Patterson didn't change, despite the carnage of the first half, was quarterbacks. Third-teamer Foster Sawyer had been given minimal reps leading up to the game, and the coaches had seen Bram Kohlhausen bring the Frogs back to the brink of an upset over mighty Oklahoma just a few weeks earlier.

"Our problem wasn't because of him," Patterson concludes. So the head coach essentially left the decision with his offensive coordinators, Meacham and Cumbie. They never blinked. They would make their stand with Bram.

Bram, meanwhile, was waiting for the word that his last chance in college football was over.

"I thought 1,000 percent I was getting benched" going into halftime, he says. But "nobody said anything.

"I think they'd had enough of Foster after the OU game. I think they just decided to roll the dice with me.

"I felt like I was in limbo. I didn't know if I was going to get pulled, or how I would get us out of this mess. I was just sitting in my locker, waiting on Coach Cumbie to come out and tell me I'm not playing football ever again.

"When they didn't say anything, I realized they weren't going to make a change. I was surprised. I wouldn't have left myself in. It was embarrassing."

"They called the quarterbacks in and Cumbie said, 'We're not doing that bad.' He looked at me and told me I needed to take care of the football. That's when I knew I was still playing. But I knew if I didn't get something going, I wouldn't be playing long. We had to score, fast and often."

• • •

After the coaches had finished with their instructions and adjustments, as the minutes ticked on toward the second half, TCU's players huddled in small position groups, pumping each other up, vowing to somehow make a game of what had already turned into an Oregon rout.

Recalls guard Bobby Thompson: "The locker room was pretty scary the first 30 seconds we were in there. It's really quiet, and we look over at the board and there's Bram going over plays.

"Coach Patterson comes in and he didn't really yell. He said, 'It is what it is. Are you guys going to lay down or go down fighting?'

"We just told each other, forget the long-term. We have to go possession-by-possession. We knew we had to score points every possession. And that's what we did.

"Being removed from it now for so long, it's still so amazing to look back and realize how mental that was, especially with Bram. I've never seen anything like it since."

Tight end Charlie Reid has a similar recollection:

At that point, in my mind, it was just like, 'Let's just go out and play,' " recalls Reid. "Logically we knew it was a slim-to-none chance that any team can come back from that. The mindset was to just go out and play the best second half we could: 'Let's go play the best we can.' You're down, whatever mistakes you'd made, correct them. Now go play a perfect second half and hope for the best. That's all you can do at that point. We knew it would take a miracle," says Reid.

"You looked at Bram and he didn't even blink. When they gave him the green light that he was staying in, that competitive spark went off in his mind. He was ready to go win.

"It didn't surprise me that he stayed in. He was a senior who had put in a lot of hard work for us. Giving him another shot was the right thing to do. Coach Patterson is always so good to the seniors. Every year his goal is to give the seniors the best year they can have. He believes in the guys. I think, with everything that happened with Bram's dad, why wouldn't you give him another shot?"

Still, the decision to keep him at quarterback had surprised Bram as much as it did most of the 65,000 people crowded into the Alamodome and those still watching at home. He has had some time to think about it in the years since:

"I think after the OU game, they knew I was a gutsy guy and that nothing really fazed me. I remember when I was younger, my All-Star Little League coach told me I was the calmest pitcher he'd ever seen. He said he'd never seen anyone walk the bases loaded and then strike out three in a row.

"It was the same in football. I was down 31-0, but I was going to attack it the same way. I didn't freak out at all the entire game. If I did, it was when it 0-0, not when it was 31-0. It was like, what can I lose? At 0-0, maybe I was tight and pressing. I think the whole team was.

"I don't remember any of the players saying much of anything to me. I felt like I was responsible for those 31 points. I didn't know what to say to anyone because I knew I didn't have the respect of the locker room like Trevone did. Everybody just kind of kept to themselves.

"I know the defense had a meeting. And Derrick Kindred [the safety who would go on to play with the Cleveland Browns] was getting everybody going, saying something like, 'This is bullshit. We're going to have to stop 'em every time.'

"Coming out, we were telling each other, we got to get our shit together. We're better than Oregon, better than this. It was so quick. We were in, then we were out. It was probably 30 minutes, but it felt like a split-second. And then it was time to play again."

Staring into his locker at halftime, Bram had reminded himself that he'd already gone through something even worse than this just two months earlier, watching his dad wither and die and not being able to do anything to stop it. He'd somehow survived that. He'd find a way to get through this as well.

"I said a prayer to him at halftime . . . 'Dude, if you're up there, you gotta bail me out on this one.' There was always a sense that he was there somewhere. I definitely thought he was watching."

Just before the Frogs were due to head back to the field, Coach Gary Patterson gathered the players around him for his final brief speech:

"All I said to the group was, on our walls at TCU, we have the programs from each bowl game we've played in, with a score. Right now, as seniors, for the rest of your life, when you walk down that hallway, that program would read Oregon 31, TCU 0. Is that what you want to see?"

As the Frogs began to move out of the locker room to start the second half, they were forced to pause for a moment. Just as they had been throughout the first half, the Ducks were a step ahead, already crowding out of their own locker room and toward the field. It was a telling moment for the Frogs, guard Bobby Thompson said:

"I remember very distinctly we were in the doorway to our locker room. The Oregon locker room was right down the hall. I'm standing next to Coach P., Josh Doctson, all of us, standing there in the front, and we can hear them in the tunnel, laughing and joking. Coach P. turns around and looks all of us dead in the face. He said, 'You listen to that. They think you're a joke. Are you going to come back and be what we say we are?' "

Chapter 11

Purple Rain

THERE WERE AT LEAST two people watching the Alamo Bowl game who weren't shocked when Bram Kohlhausen trotted out with the first-team offense after the second-half kickoff: in the stands, Fort Worth superfan Dick Lowe, and, back home in Dallas, the suspended Trevone Boykin.

Lowe, whose support had helped Patterson win the job as TCU's head coach 15 years before, would later recall that he wasn't at all surprised. "When everybody else had given up, Gary was still trying to win it. He'd come from behind before. He didn't have anything else to try."

For Boykin's part, "I knew it would be Bram immediately. The Oklahoma game, he kind of proved that he could play at this level of college football. I knew he would be the guy.

"I never doubted him. It was just getting out there and doing it," Boykin recalled later. "I talked to him [by phone] all the way leading up to the game. He was asking questions about this play or that play. I always had confidence in his ability. It was getting the opportunity. You never know until you get the opportunity."

Of course, there would have been no opportunity for

TCU

Bram and TCU faced a 31-0 deficit starting the second half of the 2016 Alamo Bowl.

Bram Kohlhausen if Trevone Boykin had stayed in their room that night in San Antonio. As Boykin talked about his backup and good friend, he couldn't help but be wistful that he hadn't been there for his teammates.

"It's always difficult when you feel you're supposed to be some place and you're not," he recalled.

"I just felt like Bram could go out and win the game. I was thinking that football is 60 minutes. People where I was were wanting to change the channel — that wasn't happening.

"We practiced together every day. I saw the ability. Bram

was very smart. He could retain information. He always had the ability to throw the ball, and we knew that in our quarterback room. I think some people fell asleep on that.

"It wasn't that they weren't moving the ball, or he was making mistakes on offense. There was a bunch of young guys playing who had never played before. There were guys who hadn't played all year playing in this game. For me, there wasn't a problem on offense. It was just getting it going.

"When their starting quarterback went down, I figured it would be a new game. Vernon Adams is a great dual-threat guy. He could run, throw, make plays with his feet. I'm sure he got all the reps, and when he went down, they may not have been ready for that adjustment. TCU was."

• • •

It wasn't until the Frogs' offense trotted out for the first series of the second half that fans in the stands realized Bram Kohlhausen was still in at quarterback. There was an audible rumble as this realization sank into the collective consciousness. This guy again? What in the world was Gary Patterson thinking?

The answer to that question was almost too simple to believe: Gary Patterson wasn't thinking about it at all.

Like most successful major-college head football coaches, Patterson is most comfortable when he's making decisions about virtually every facet of the game. He trusts no one as much as he trusts himself. But he's smart enough to understand that his real expertise is on the defensive side of the ball — so his insistence on control ends at the offense.

Thus, by his own choice, Patterson had zero input into whether Bram would remain at quarterback to start the second half. He delegated that decision entirely to his two offensive coordinators, Doug Meacham and Sonny Cumbie. The offense was theirs; Patterson would not interfere. Besides, he already had his hands full just trying to fix the disaster that was his defense in the first half.

"We talked about it briefly at halftime," Cumbie says, "and between Coach Meacham and I, there was no hesitation to leave Bram in. Being a bowl game and that Bram was the No. 2 quarterback, he'd really had a lot of reps. We just thought, give him a shot, give him a chance to get into a rhythm, get this game going. He'd done a great job of sparking us in the second half of the Oklahoma game. We knew he had it in him. Foster [Sawyer] hadn't gotten many reps. It was Bram's last game, and we just decided to ride it out."

Meacham and Cumbie had decided as well that they would hold nothing back from their extensive bag of tricks. They would pull out all the stops.

They also understood that in the end it would come down to the players and their execution. That, not the game plan, had been the team's biggest failure in the first half: Too many mistakes. Too many penalties.

"It wasn't that Bram was playing bad," says Meacham. "One, Oregon was scoring a lot; and two, we really weren't challenging them that much. We were playing kind of guarded.

"We just said, let's open the damn playbook up and call better plays. We just started calling it a lot looser, not just playing not to mess up but playing to win it. We said to each other, let's just let 'er rip.

"So we came out and ran a trick play on the first play of the second half and hit it. We just kind of started doing what we do."

• • •

The Frogs' first offensive play was a beauty called Black Mamba, and it was as exotic as it sounds. The Frogs had run it on the second play of the game against Ole Miss a year earlier and hit it for a touchdown.

But that was with Boykin at quarterback. This time Kohlhausen took the snap in the shotgun, stutter-stepped forward, then turned and fired a pass *behind the line of scrimmage* to freshman wide receiver Tony Brooks-James out on the left flank.

Brooks-James, who would move to defensive back the following year, had caught just two passes during the entire regular season. He had never even practiced the play in which he essentially became a second quarterback.

"Sonny had gotten that play the year before from a high school coach named Hal Wasson [Southlake Carroll, Corsicana]," Meacham recalls. "I called the play thinking Kolby Listenbee was out there. I look over and he's standing next to me. I said, 'What are you doing here?' "

Brooks-James caught Kohlhausen's lateral pass behind two blockers and ran the play perfectly, throwing his own pass to running back Aaron Green cutting across the middle. It went for 20 yards and a first down, just TCU's sixth in the game.

After that, Kohlhausen would go three-for-three in a 10-play, 69-yard drive that culminated in a 24-yard Jaden Oberkrom field goal.

It was just three points — the Frogs still trailed 31-3, a seemingly impossible mountain to climb — but it was as if the dark cloud hanging over TCU had lifted and the sun had come out.

Says Bram: "I just knew we needed to score, and when we did, even just a field goal, it took a weight off our shoulders. We needed a good drive, just put some points on the board at that point. There was just a good feeling that we'd moved the ball down the field like that. We'd had so many three-and-outs in the first half. You could feel the energy after that. Now we felt we had to score again."

In the television booth, former Texas coach Mack Brown had already resisted his ESPN producers' suggestion of talking about the impact an Oregon rout and a TCU shellacking would have on their respective programs. As a veteran head coach, he knew the vagaries of the game all too well; he'd lived both sides of that coin. After Oberkrom's field goal, he told the TV audience he'd agreed with the play call and floated a thought that TCU fans watching at home had not dared even to consider:

"You've got to get some points. They've had nothing happen positive in the game. Get the points. We're seeing a more comfortable quarterback. I promise you this will help the defense play better. It gives them hope."

Hope? Really? Just a sliver, maybe, a fleeting whisper in the deepest recess of the brain, but there all the same.

Hope.

• • •

When the Frogs' defense held Oregon to a three-and-out on the Ducks' next possession, a series that included yet another bad snap between the second-team center and backup quarterback Lockie, it was as if ESPN's Brown could sense what was about to happen.

"I'm telling you," he told his audience, "you don't want momentum to change with a bunch of young people. It's hard to get it turned back."

The Frogs knew that they had to score on every possession — and that they couldn't keep settling for field goals. Two plays into their next drive — a three-yard loss by Aaron Green and a dropped pass by Shaun Nixon — TCU faced a critical third-and-13 at their own 33.

Kohlhausen hit sophomore wide receiver Emanuel Porter five yards short of the first-down yardage. Somehow Porter split two defenders, found daylight down the right sideline and darted for 25 yards. It was the Frogs' first third-down conversion in nine tries.

Kohlhausen would finish off an 11-play, 64-yard drive with a desperation fourth-and-five play from the Oregon 26, lofting a pass over two leaping defenders and into the hands of freshman Jaelan Austin in the end zone.

With the extra point, TCU had cut it to 31-10.

Though the gap was still daunting, for tight end Charlie Reid, it was the moment he and a handful of teammates began to believe the Frogs might actually have a chance to pull this off. The feeling in the Frogs' huddle, the confidence emanating from Bram Kohlhausen, was electric, almost intoxicating.

"The touchdown pass to Jaelan Austin," Reid recalls, "it was like, 'Wow, he's rolling!' And [the Ducks] were having so much trouble with their center and their quarterback, it was like, 'If this is happening, it's happening now. Let's take advantage.'

"That was the spark. It got things rolling again. You could see Bram get fired up. He was ready to rock and roll. We all thought, if he's ready to rock, let's all get ready to rock."

That spark of hope flared even higher when TCU freshman Arico Evans forced a Ducks fumble on the ensuing kickoff and walk-on safety Michael Downing recovered for the Frogs at the Oregon 16-yard line.

"When we get the field goal, there's a sense of relief," recalls Cumbie. "But after we cut it to 31-10 and they fumbled on the kickoff, that put everything in a different perspective."

Coach Meacham's recollection echoes his colleague's:

"Even [after the first touchdown] there was no shape or form that we were thinking about winning. It just made us feel better. Then we kick off and they fumble . . . Now, suddenly, we are thinking about winning.

"Their backup center couldn't snap it, and their backup quarterback wasn't very good. We were driving on every possession and started wearing their defense out."

The crowd, rising to its feet, felt it, too. The atmosphere had completely changed, on both sides of the field. The electricity was palpable, as if a shimmering St. Elmo's fire was crackling and flying off the walls of the arena. The hair on the back of Gareth Kohlhausen's neck began to stand up. What the hell was happening?

Both teams were now playing without their No. 1 quarterback and starting centers. TCU's All-American and future first-round draft pick, wide receiver Josh Doctson, had not even suited up. The Frogs were playing freshmen (Turpin, Austin, Brooks-James and Nixon) and a sophomore (Porter) at wideout. The explosive Turpin would also soon be limping to the sideline.

Back in Dallas, Trevone Boykin completely forgot about his domino game and focused on the TV set.

• • •

The TCU crowd, originally cowed by the first-half whipping the Ducks had administered, was now howling like a wild animal. There was a sudden realization that the Ducks, struggling with simply getting the ball snapped, might just be catchable after all.

In the TV booth, an excited Mack Brown was expanding on his original prescient observation: "Momentum's a powerful thing, especially with young people. When it's working, you can't stop 'em. When it turns, you have trouble turning it back. The Oregon defense has to move, has to make a play, knock the ball loose. They gotta get a stop here."

After the fumble and TCU's recovery on the Oregon 16, simply holding TCU to a field goal at this point would have been a major victory for the Ducks. It would have cost the Frogs valuable clock time and a precious opportunity. But Bram Kohlhausen was not to be denied.

Facing a precarious third-and-nine from the Oregon 15, Kohlhausen rolled left and saw the entire field open up in front of him. He tucked the ball and raced for the end zone. At the 1-yard line, Oregon's Khalil Oliver flipped him head over heels. The hit was hard enough to knock the wind out of him, but it was first and goal at the 1.

Stunned and winded, Kohlhausen walked slowly to the sideline while redshirt freshman Foster Sawyer came in to complete a pass to Turpin for no gain. Then Kohlhausen was back in. Two straight runs by Aaron Green against the stiffening Oregon defense lost a yard. Another fourth down, another make-or-break play for the Frogs.

Kohlhausen retreated to pass on fourth-and-2, again saw an opening and dashed around left end, diving between two defenders into the end zone. Then the kick by Oberkrom chopped Oregon's lead to 14.

In the stands, fans were beginning to grasp how the landscape of the game had transformed.

"Bram had already had a couple of fourth-down conversions, and he took it into the end zone and scored," says his friend Luke Schreiner. "Oregon had lost its quarterback. TCU had all the momentum at that point. We realized that they not only had a chance to make it close, they could win it. Now it was just a matter of whether they had enough time."

That was the point at which Zach Mafrige also knew TCU meant business:

"I remember very well, when Bram started doing the James Harden celebration where you're cooking" — the NBA star's trademark "stirring the pot" gesture after scoring — "that they weren't going down without a fight."

Thirty-six seconds remained in the third quarter, and the Frogs were now just two touchdowns away from catching the Ducks. Bram Kohlhausen had taken over the game.

ESPN play-by-play announcer Dave Flemming was on board, exclaiming: "You can see why TCU stuck with this kid. There's just an entirely different feel."

After the Ducks' offense had snapped it 50 times in the first half, 26 of them in the second quarter, Oregon had run only five third-quarter offensive plays. TCU had dominated the third-quarter time of possession, 12:26 to 2:34 for Oregon.

On ESPN, Mack Brown summed it up: "What a great third quarter for TCU. They've turned it around, and now we have us a ballgame for the fourth."

• • •

Emotions were at fever pitch among the TCU fans as the fateful fourth quarter got under way. But four plays in, the Ducks suddenly silenced the roaring TCU fans with a play that could have extinguished the Frogs' flashfire of momentum in an instant.

On a third-and-4 play from the TCU 45, Oregon QB Lockie squatted to scoop up another low snap from backup center Doug Brenner. The Ducks' quarterback flicked a pass to wide receiver Darren Carrington, who was slicing through the Frogs' secondary from the left side. Catching the pass on a dead sprint, Carrington split two TCU defenders and raced 45 yards for an apparent Oregon touchdown. Shell-shocked Ducks fans leaped to their feet. The TCU crowd groaned. This would be the final dagger, they were sure.

But, as he'd knelt to corral the low snap, Lockie's right knee had touched the Alamodome's artificial turf. The back judge saw it instantly, waving off the score. Replay confirmed that Lockie was down 5 yards behind the line of scrimmage. The Ducks had no choice but to punt.

Oregon punter Ian Wheeler did his part, pinning the Frogs inside their own 10-yard line at the 7.

Not even that could slow TCU down. The Frogs embarked on a 76-yard drive whose key play was straight out of Bram's high-school highlight reel. On third-and-3 from his own 14, he took the snap and then retreated as if he intended to surprise the Ducks with a quick pooch kick. It was a play that was actually in the Frogs' playbook, and the situation was ripe for it.

But, as Kohlhausen dashed to his right as if to get a running start for the kick, he spotted an open Aaron Green. His pass hit Green on the run for 36 yards, taking the Frogs to midfield.

"It was just like something off his high-school tapes," big brother Gareth recalls. "That was his play, moving to his right, and he hit a big pass . . . and they go from deep in their own territory to the 50. That's when I think we truly began to believe that this could happen. It was like 'OK, they can do this.' "

A 21-yard Kohlhausen completion to Jarrison Stewart helped the Frogs reach the Oregon 13, but a subsequent third-down sack by Tyson Coleman rattled the ball loose from Bram's hands. TCU tailback Kyle Hicks pounced on the loose football at the 17. It was another of those karma-tinged plays that could have easily killed the Frogs' momentum and left them short of time at the end. Instead, they salvaged 3 points on Oberkrom's 34-yard field goal, his second of the day. Every Frogs player and fan looked to the scoreboard: *31-20, Oregon.*

"Now it's game on," recalls Cumbie. "Now you're a stop away from making it a one- or two-score game. Now guys started believing. They're thinking, 'We can come back; we can win this game!' That was huge."

Getting only 3 points out of the long drive, however, left the Frogs in a daunting position. Yes, it was now a two-score game, but TCU would have to follow up a touchdown with a challenging 2-point conversion to put themselves in position to tie the game with a field goal.

There could no mental mistakes, no turnovers, no possessions without points, no clock-eating drives by Oregon. Everything had to go perfectly for the Frogs to capitalize on their one slim chance.

• • •

It didn't make TCU fans feel any easier when the Frogs' surprise onside kick was recovered by the Ducks at TCU's 45-yard line. Seven minutes and 45 seconds remained on the clock. Any Oregon score — even a couple of first downs — would likely doom the Frogs.

But Patterson's defense, which had played so poorly in the first half, was rising to the occasion now. The Frogs' defenders were giving the Ducks' laboring defense no chance to catch its breath and regroup. Patterson's ferocious black shirts quickly ushered Lockie and his offense to another three-and-out, and Oregon punted again inside the TCU 10.

Kohlhausen calmly kick-started the Frogs' offense with a 19-yard completion to Shaun Nixon. On the next play the Frogs' quarterback scrambled for 9 yards but paid for the gain by taking a sharp hit to the left rib cage from Oregon's Rodney Hardrick. Again Bram wobbled to the sidelines, flanked by two TCU trainers. The clock showed 6 minutes to play. Sawyer came on to run one play — TCU was penalized for holding — and Kohlhausen, ignoring the pain that pierced his side every time he took a breath, raced back onto the field.

"Fifth-year senior," Mack Brown informed his listeners from the booth, expounding on the quarterback's determination to ignore his injury and get back into play. "He's been waiting for this opportunity since he went to Houston five years ago. Get healthy the rest of your life."

Starting from his own 27, Kohlhausen now methodically connected on one pass, then another and another — a pair to freshman Jaelan Austin for 8 and then 29 yards, and another to sophomore Emanuel Porter for 16.

Kohlhausen also sandwiched in a quarterback draw for 4 yards and a crucial first down. His only incompletion, inten ded for Porter in the end zone, drew a flag on Ducks cornerback Chris Seisay for obvious pass interference, setting TCU up with a first down at the Oregon 2.

With a hair more than 3 1/2 minutes left to play and the crowd in an absolute uproar, Bram Kohlhausen seemed to grasp that, for this one time in his life, for whatever reason, he really was destiny's child. The hesitation that had kept him from taking charge on that crucial play at Oklahoma two months earlier was gone. This time he boldly took matters into his own hands with a decision that had TCU coaches screaming on the sideline.

"The play call was a quarterback sweep to the right that had been designed with Trevone in mind," Bram recalls. Tailback Aaron Green "was cussing the coaches in the huddle. He was in his hometown and wanted to score a touchdown."

Always a players' quarterback, Bram made a split-second decision that stunned his coaches. The Frogs would run the play, but not as designed with Bram carrying the ball.

Instead, in the huddle Kohlhausen instructed Green to take the snap on the sweep to the right, the short side of the field. Instead of Bram toting the football, his cooked-up sandlot call had him taking on Green's role, leading the blocking.

It was reckless. It was daring. Most of all, though, it showed Bram's mindset. He was taking charge, and he was taking care of his teammates. It was important to Aaron Green to score in this game, in his hometown. Changing the play call to make that happen would be deemed either incredibly foolish or brazenly bold, depending on its success or failure. Either way, Bram was taking the responsibility.

"The only people who knew what we were doing was me, Aaron and the center," Bram recalls.

"When he saw Aaron line up on the left side, Coach Meacham was running down the sideline, trying to call a timeout, not realizing Aaron was going to shift over and take the snap. But the official didn't see [the coach], and the play went off."

Kohlhausen, who was in that zone that only elite athletes know, didn't just lead the sweep, he executed a perfect cut block on Oregon defensive end Eddie Heard, putting him on the ground. Green squeezed around the pileup and just inside the pylon for the touchdown that brought TCU to within 5 points of the reeling Ducks.

"I blocked the defensive end, and Aaron turned the corner and scored," Bram says.

On the sideline, TCU's stunned offensive coaches swallowed their hearts and the curses on the tips of their tongues.

"I was jumping up and down on the sideline because I saw the running back was lined up on the wrong side," Coach Meacham says. "We hadn't practiced it that way ever. Bram goes over, does a cut block on their D-end and puts him on his back. Bram played so tough. He was playing for something. He played like he had something inside him, motivating him to play. I thought he played out of his mind. It was unbelievable."

The contrast between the first and second halves was eye-popping. With Vernon Adams at quarterback in the first half, Oregon had racked up 345 yards and scored 31 points. With Adams in street clothes on the sideline in the second half, the

Ducks had 49 yards and zero points. Conversely, Bram Kohlhausen had pulled a Hyde-to-Jekyll transformation, going from impotent to unstoppable.

"Bram made some phenomenal throws on that drive," Coach Cumbie says. "Bram and Aaron Green basically made up a play on the field. We just seized the momentum on all three sides of the football."

• • •

With just 3:32 to play, the situation now mandated that the Frogs go for the 2-point conversion that would potentially bring them to within a field goal of tying the score. But TCU had a problem: Kohlhausen had again been forced to retreat to the sideline, this time with severe cramps in both legs. Third-teamer Sawyer would have to execute this extraordinarily crucial play. If it failed, TCU would have to score a touchdown to win. If it succeeded, the Frogs could settle for a field goal to tie.

Inspired by Bram's moxie, Meacham and Cumbie reached deep into their bag of tricks and called "Outback," a fake option left reverse pass by redshirt freshman wide receiver Shaun Nixon. It was a call that meant the play's success or failure would not be riding on third-string quarterback Sawyer. The Ducks' defense bit on the reverse, believing Nixon intended to run it. Instead, Nixon, on the run to his right, flipped a soft pass to tight end Buck Jones, who had leaked out and was wide open in the right side of the end zone.

TCU had now cut the once-impossible 31-0 deficit to 31-28. They needed a stop and one final miracle to win or to send the game into overtime.

As Oregon prepared to start from its own 9-yard line after excellent kickoff coverage by TCU, ESPN sideline reporter Allison Williams was telling her viewers how fired up Gary Patterson was. Before the 2-point conversion, she revealed, he'd turned to her and yelled, "This is what it's like to play with a backup quarterback!"

Ominously, though, Williams also reported that "about five trainers" were attending to Kohlhausen on the sideline training table.

The Ducks, by now severely rattled, played right into TCU's hands. Instead of trying to eat up clock time, Lockie threw wildly high and incomplete on consecutive passes on second and third down, stopping the clock twice and preserving precious seconds for TCU. The ensuing short punt from Oregon's 10-yard line and Desmon White's 9-yard return set the Frogs up at the Ducks' 36. They were already arguably within Oberkrom's kicking range, and Kohlhausen came off the training table and onto the field.

A few vocal TCU fans had already grown impatient with the Frogs' methodical offense during their second-half comeback, loudly urging the quarterback to get the plays off quicker. Bram heard them but was implacable. Facing a short field and a chance to put the game away with a touchdown, Meacham and Cumbie turned ultra-conservative.

Whatever happened now, they knew the Frogs had to come out of this drive at least with the game-tying field goal. Then, riding the crest of the wave of momentum, they would take their chances in OT.

Kohlhausen completed a 5-yard pass to Nixon on first down, and then it was all Aaron Green. Five straight runs brought the Frogs to a third-and-1 play at the Oregon 5-yard line, where TCU took its final timeout.

Then Kohlhausen rolled right, saw Austin covered in the end zone and threw the ball away to stop the clock.

"We had a good play called," says Bram; "it was another rub, or pick play, and it was just covered up by Oregon's D. I just threw the ball out of bounds and lived for overtime. The thinking on that drive was that we already had points" — the all-but-guaranteed field goal — "and with the momentum we had, going into overtime was in our favor.

"I remember getting on the headset with Coach Cumbie and him basically telling me that we were in field-goal range, and I needed to take care of the football. The running backs coach, Coach Luper, was preaching to the running backs to take care of the football. So we were just going to take care of the football, and if we break a touchdown, that was great, but if we go to overtime, we had the advantage there, too."

"It was a good feeling to know we had Jaden, one of the best college football kickers of all time. I figured he would drill it."

As Oberkrom lined up the kick, the fact that the game rested in the hands – or foot – of the best kicker in NCAA football didn't keep Kohlhausen from turning and staring into the stands, too nervous to watch.

Picking up on Kohlhausen's nervousness, Mack Brown chuckled to his TV audience: "I've been there. I've said a few 'Please, Lord's."

Then Oberkrom knocked through the gimme 22-yard field goal to tie the score with 19 seconds left. The frenetic TCU crowd was going bananas. The Frogs had somehow crawled out of that 31-point grave. Up to that point, the biggest comeback in bowl history had been Texas Tech's rally from a 38-7 deficit against Minnesota in the 2007 Insight Bowl to win 44-41 in overtime. Now TCU was approaching that territory.

• • •

Bram insists today that, when he turned away from the field for the kick, he wasn't saying any silent prayers but was simply focusing on the scoreboard to see how much time Oregon would have left on the clock. He was still taking nothing for granted. It turned out he had ample reason to worry.

In the TV booth, Mack Brown surveyed the field as the camera focused on the ever-dangerous Oregon kick-returner Charles Nelson. "I'll tell you this," Brown promised, "they're not going to kick it to this guy; it'll be a squib kick to a big guy."

It was one of the few times Brown was wrong on arguably the best afternoon any college football color analyst ever had. Oberkrom's kickoff went straight to Nelson a yard deep in his own end zone. Good coverage would have made the decision look brilliant and left the Ducks needing a long drive to get within field goal range. Poor coverage, though, made it look like a brain-dead move. Nelson squirted through the first wave of TCU defenders, broke a tackle and was finally pulled down at the Oregon 48.

Play-by-play announcer Dave Flemming was almost screaming: "Why would you do that? Oregon has a timeout left. They can throw a pass downfield and then kick a field goal to win it!"

Would TCU's incredible comeback from 31 points down be wiped out by this inexplicable coaching blunder? If the Frogs lost, would Patterson's career be forever tarnished because he'd put the game in the hands of his special-teams kick-off coverage?

Patterson's choices were clear: Kick deep, hope to pin the Ducks back in their own end of the field and rely on his defense to hold and send the game into overtime; or attempt the squib kick, which would cut down the chances of a long return but would almost certainly guarantee a shorter field for Oregon. The wild card in the mix was the dangerously talented Nelson.

"I was extremely nervous here," Bram says. "I was getting

my calf cramp worked on and just heard Oregon's fans erupt. Oregon is so explosive, when I heard the Oregon fans cheering, I was asking the trainers what happened, and they were giving me a play-by-play."

Patterson was beside himself on the sideline. TV lip-readers could plainly see him excoriating his kickoff team's defenders, disgustedly screaming "What was that?" as TCU's special-teams players came off the field, heads down.

Nineteen seconds remained. If the Ducks could hit something downfield for 20 yards or so, they would be within makeable field goal range.

On first down, Lockie retreated, looking downfield for an open receiver, but the Frogs had every option blanketed. Lockie was forced to dump the ball to running back Royce Freeman, who was pushed out of bounds at the TCU 46 with just 2 seconds to play.

That was way too long for a field goal attempt. No time to do anything but throw up a Hail Mary. Lockie never even got the chance: TCU defensive end Terrell Lathan took care of that with a sack as time expired in regulation.

The Frogs had done exactly what they vowed they would do at halftime: score on every possession (three touchdowns and three field goals) and hold Oregon to zero points. The Ducks had totaled 52 offensive yards in the second half, with their longest play going for only 8.

For TCU now, there was just one thing left on the to-do list: Finish the job.

Chapter 12
Overtime

Great occasions do not make heroes or cowards;
they simply unveil them to the eyes of men.
Brooke Foss Westcott

OVERTIME DID NOT FRIGHTEN TCU. It was what they'd prayed for, what they'd played for, throughout their incredible second-half comeback. When you've returned from the scoreboard dead, you don't flinch at the opportunity to play a little longer. Overtime was the opportunity to finish the job.

Yes, it would have been sweet to have put the game away in regulation. But the Frogs were clearly feeling great about themselves and their chances, having dominated the second half so thoroughly and built up such a powerful tsunami of momentum.

Not that Gary Patterson would for even a moment countenance any letup or allow himself or his players to suffer the idea that this game was somehow in the bag. He'd stride the sidelines in a pink tutu before that happened. But, as Mack Brown had told TV viewers in the third quarter, confidence is everything in young athletes. They need to believe there's a chance. And over the previous 30 minutes of play, the Frogs had proven something to themselves and everyone watching: that they not only belonged on the field with Oregon but, at this time, on this day, were the better team.

The Frogs' belief in themselves had been shattered in the Ducks' ferocious march to that 31-0 halftime lead. But now the architect of most of that damage — quarterback Vernon Adams — was standing on the sideline in street clothes.

Oregon's vulnerability in its lack of depth behind Adams at quarterback, as well at a critical position like center, where everything begins, had been excruciatingly exposed. That wasn't going to change in overtime.

Beyond any of Oregon's troubles, however, was the Frogs' blossoming faith in their own backup quarterback, Bram Kohlhausen.

What Adams had done to TCU in the first half, Kohlhausen had reciprocated against Oregon in the second. In those two quarters he'd ripped the Ducks' defense to shreds, completing 16 of 21 passes for 248 yards and a touchdown while also running the ball eight times for 41 yards and two TDs. He had become the physical and emotional leader that, with Trevone Boykin out of the picture, TCU so desperately craved.

"The presence that Bram had with us, not many people are going to be able to do that, have a cool head and really command a team," said guard Bobby Thompson. "Everything that could go wrong went wrong, and not just in the first half, but even earlier in the season and that week, too . . . his dad dying, what happened to Trevone.

"I'll never forget: The second half begins, we're losing 31-0, it's do-or-die."

Most of the doing had already been done as the Frogs

dug out from the 31-point avalanche that had buried them in the first half. The Frogs had one goal now: For the first time, let the Ducks know what it felt like to be behind in this game.

• • •

Kohlhausen and the Frogs were delighted when Oregon won the overtime toss but elected to put TCU's offense on the field first.

"This drive was extremely important," says Bram, "because we had to score. This would be the first time Oregon was down the entire game, and we needed to put the Ducks in that position."

Since 1996, when the current college overtime rules were implemented, the goal is to get the game finished as quickly as possible while mandating that each team has the same opportunity. An overtime period is a two-possession series, with each team getting one offensive possession each, beginning at their opponent's 25-yard line. Teams start within easy field-goal range.

Kohlhausen, utilizing a play originally designed for the speedy and elusive Boykin, authored TCU's first big strike in overtime on second-and-7. He dropped back as if to pass, then pulled the ball down and hip-danced up the center of the field for 11 yards and a first down at the Oregon 11.

"This was an option play designed for Trevone," Bram says. "The Oregon defensive ends would peel with the backs when they swung out. If the defensive end does not take the running back, we throw a swing pass. If the defensive end takes the running back, which he did in this case, I run the draw. It was a matter of reading the defensive end, and I was able to outrun a few guys and get a first down."

Remember the Bram Kohlhausen who didn't feel confident enough to call his own late-game play against Oklahoma earlier that season? That guy no longer existed, as he'd already proven in the fourth quarter by switching roles with Aaron Green on the Frogs' final touchdown in regulation. Now he was reading the Oregon defense and reacting instinctually.

After Green punched through the left side for 4 yards, Kohlhausen threw slightly behind sophomore Emanuel Porter, breaking from right to left across the end zone. Porter, who wasn't even listed on the team's depth chart, somehow reached back, snatched the ball out of a defensive back's face and handed TCU its first lead of the game.

"He made a great catch, just unbelievable," Bram marvels. "I threw it behind him, [but] he just slowed down and went and got it like a basketball rebound."

With the PAT, TCU finally had a lead: 38-31. Now the Ducks had to respond with their own touchdown or watch the Frogs celebrate. After its surrender to the Frogs' second-half siege, could the Oregon offense show any sign of life?

The answer to that question was slow in coming, but come it eventually did. After a couple of runs for a combined 6 yards and a Jeff Lockie incompletion, the Ducks faced their own do-or-die moment with a fourth-and-4 play at the TCU 19.

A desperate Lockie found running back Royce Freeman, who would lead all rushers for the game with 130 yards on 26 carries, swinging out of the backfield for a 17-yard romp to the TCU 2. It was easily the Ducks' longest play since the first half. Freeman gouged out a yard, then slammed into the line again on second-and-goal from the 1. It appeared as if TCU's stiff defensive front had stopped him cold, but 290-pound guard Jake Pisarcik, rumbling in from behind Freeman, pushed the pile forward and across the goal line.

The PAT tied it at 38-38, triggering the second overtime.

• • •

With the suspense ratcheted up to an even higher pitch, this time the Ducks got the first crack on offense.

Oregon lost 2 yards on three plays but then salvaged 3 points on Aidan Schneider's 44-yard field goal, edging the score to 41-38.

Oregon had reclaimed the lead, but if TCU could score another touchdown, it would be over.

The key play in TCU's series was its first one. Tony Brooks-James was wide open with plenty of running room, but Kohlhausen, unable to set his feet, threw high over the middle and just out of reach of the leaping Brooks-James.

A long pass intended for Emanuel Porter in the end zone was also incomplete, and Porter limped off with a leg cramp. Oregon blitzed on third down, forcing Kohlhausen to dump it short to Hicks, who took a 3-yard loss. Oberkrom's 46-yard field-goal kick was true, to tie it again at 41-all.

"I've watched the game replays a thousand times and usually skip the second overtime period because so little happened for either team," Bram says. "On the first-down play I really screwed up.

"We ran a double-move rub route for the outside wide receiver, and he was wide open. Tony James probably would have scored if I'd given him a catchable ball. I had a few offensive linemen at my feet and was not able to make an accurate throw. It was high over the middle, and I honestly thought someone was going to intercept it.

"Luckily it fell incomplete, and we were able to settle for the field goal."

The game was now into its third overtime.

• • •

This time, TCU didn't even bother going to the air. Instead, the Frogs relentlessly punished Oregon's fatigued defensive front. In just two plays, TCU had slugged its way to the Oregon 8-yard line: Aaron Green burst up the middle for 12 yards on first down, then slashed off right tackle for another 5.

Fittingly, it now came down to Kohlhausen. On third down from the Oregon 8, Kohlhausen ran a perfect option play around right end. With Green trailing, Kohlhausen read Ducks defensive end Tyson Coleman like a comic book. Faced with a choice, Coleman did what he had to do, peeling off to take Green. That left an opening for Kohlhausen to squeeze into the end zone as tackle Joseph Noteboom sealed off pursuit from the inside.

"During the option play, the defensive end was playing both myself and Green," Bram recalls. "I could hear Green saying 'no, no, no,' because he did not want me to pitch the ball. I stretched the option out as long as possible, then faked a pitch and tried to get as many yards as I could around the end. I thought there would be a linebacker to take me out on the sideline, so, while anticipating a hit when I turned the corner, I got a little off-balance because there was nobody around the end."

On the mandated 2-point conversion attempt, Bram rolled to his right, looking in the end zone for Tony Brooks-James. Throwing across his body, Kohlhausen bounced the ball at Austin's feet.

"The play was covered up, so it was on me to make a play with my feet or my arm. I scrambled around a little bit, and Tony James leaked out and was wide open. I made another off-balance throw, and it went straight into the dirt. Coach Meacham would call that a 'dirt ball.'

"I felt horrible, because it was a layup and would have put TCU and the defense in a great position. Oregon would have had to score and get the 2-point play to win."

Now TCU led by only 6, 47-41. It would come down to TCU's defense against Oregon's mortally wounded offense, a mismatch since the second half began.

Under pressure on first down, Lockie threw for Darren Carrington in the left corner of the end zone. TCU defensive back Corry O'Meally knocked it away.

Then, on second down, Royce Freeman, basically all the offense the Ducks had in the second half, banged over the middle for 8 yards, setting the Ducks up with an easily makeable third-and-2 play at the TCU 17.

But on third down Lockie dropped the snap. He snatched it up just in time to get hammered by linebacker Ty Summers for a 6-yard loss.

That left one last gasp for the Ducks . . . and Lockie's scrambling make-or-break pass on fourth down was tipped away at the end zone by Frogs junior safety Denzel Johnson.

The TCU Horned Frogs had defeated the Oregon Ducks, 47-41, in triple overtime!

• • •

The roar from the astounded Frogs fans rippled across south Texas in a wave that threatened to blow the roof off the Alamodome. By the time the deflected ball had hit the ground, the pent-up Frogs had exploded into an unprecedented celebration.

A triumphant Johnson sprinted down the field, signaling "incomplete" as he goose-stepped to the 50, trailed by jubilant teammates. TCU players ran in circles, too elated to think straight. TCU's second-half magic carpet ride had reached its zenith.

Bram and one of the team managers raced across the field with the orange Gatorade bucket, dumping it on Gary Patterson's back just as he reached Oregon head coach Mark

Helfrich for the traditional post-game handshake. Patterson flinched but never even looked back.

Outside the stands, sports channels from the airwaves to the internet lit up like a decade's worth of Fourth of Julys rolled into one. "Wow, greatest comeback in Bowl history," tweeted ESPN's Kirk Herbstreit. "Bram Kohlhausen is a stud — good for him."

The moment is still vivid to Bram:

"It was like, 'Holy shit, what just happened!!?? What do I do next?' I just grabbed all my buddies and gave 'em hugs. I grabbed an Alamo Bowl championship T-shirt, took off my pads and put it on. Everybody was just running around, finding someone to grab."

Unbeknownst to Bram, the one person he most wanted to hug — his mom — was also caught up in the melee on the field, searching for her son. Dash Kohlhausen had intercepted a disgruntled Oregon booster who was leaving the field and offered a hundred bucks for the departing fan's sideline pass. He'd slipped the pass to his mother, knowing how much it would mean to her and to his kid brother if they could be together at this moment. Of course, the sideline pass didn't technically allow her to be on the field, but it got her close enough to slip into the celebration unnoticed.

Bram was about to be named the game's MVP. He'd grabbed a phone from an equipment manager to call his family, but the Kohlhausen crew had been using their phones so much during the game that their batteries were all dead. Bram had no idea where his family might be, so he asked someone from the team to help him look for his mom.

"ESPN wanted an interview, but I told them, 'No, I'm looking for my family right now.' They were about to hold the trophy presentation. When I turned around to go to the stage, my mom was standing right there. We grabbed each other and hugged, and we both broke down in tears. She was already crying, so it was hard not to."

Donna Kohlhausen remembers those tears vividly: "When we saw each other, Bram immediately scooped me up in his arms and hugged me and we were both crying together. I think it was because Bill wasn't there. He was so devoted to Bram. I just wished he had lived to see this. He would have been so excited."

Bram will be the first to say that he's confident his dad saw every play and, wherever he might be, celebrated as wildly and happily as anyone on the field that day.

When the Frogs were lighting victory cigars in the locker room later, Bram could not stop smiling.

Bill Kohlhausen always loved a good cigar.

Chapter 13

Full Circle

YEARS LATER, Julie Baker, the Alamo Bowl's vice president of operations, still winces about the breakdown in security that had allowed Donna Kohlhausen to find her way onto the field after the game. Yet it had led to what was likely the most emotional moment of the evening. Baker couldn't help but be touched as she watched mother and son find each other just before the trophy presentation.

"I did see him hug her," Baker says. "I don't think I'll ever forget that moment."

It was certainly a night the Kohlhausen family will never forget. In large ways and small, that extraordinary game changed their lives, from the moment they left the field for after-game steaks and champagne in the plush surroundings of Morton's Steak House.

"When we walked in," Gareth says, "there were fans from both teams who stood and cheered."

"It was incredibly emotional," recalls family friend Susan Hunt, "because Bill had just passed away. We knew Bill was looking down, probably with his hand on Bram's shoulder. I think he was elated and so proud."

When Gareth talks about his little brother's path to that triumphal game, he likes to remember that bet he made with Bram back in the UH days. Concerned about Bram's prospects, he'd hoped to motivate Bram to leave the University of Houston by betting him $1,000 he'd never have the nerve to do it. Sure enough, when Bram committed to enrolling at L.A. Harbor, Gareth ponied up $500; he paid the other $500 shortly after his little brother moved to Redondo Beach.

It turned out to be a profitable investment.

"I made it back on the Alamo Bowl," Gareth says.

"I'd bet $500 when the betting line was TCU plus 1. Then, when it was announced that Bram would be starting, the line went to TCU plus 7. I figured if I believed in them with 1 point, I had to bet on my brother with 7. Then at halftime – and I knew our dad would tell me it was a fool's bet, but I had to do it anyway – it was 'pick'em,' meaning it started 0-0 and it was whoever won the second half. Plus, I took the scoring line for another $200. I think I wound up winning around two grand."

• • •

Today, working in real estate at Latipac Commercial in Houston, Gareth still relishes telling anyone who will listen about that magical night in San Antonio.

So does Donna Kohlhausen, who remains fiercely proud of what her youngest son accomplished that night in San Antonio.

"Bram would do anything to win the game that day," she says proudly. "He was not going to lose."

The game, and Bram's role in it, remains a thrilling memory not just for Bram's family but for his friends.

"It's still surreal to me," says Bram's TCU teammate Charlie Reid, former Frogs tight end and now the strength coach at Fort Worth's All Saints Episcopal School.

"It was the best football game I've ever been a part of in my entire life, period. Bram is such a dear friend of mine. I felt so proud of him. He'd come back from such adversity, his dad's death, starting that game after Trevone was sent home, being down 31-0 at the half. A lot of people don't believe in miracles, but if that's not a miracle, I don't know what you'd call it."

Bram's buddy Luke Schreiner, now the head ranch manager at his family-owned property, the YO Schreiner Ranch in Kerrville, had attended the game with Kerrville friends Riley Miller and Charlie Kinnison. It was Miller who woke up the morning after the trio had joined the Kohlhausen party at Morton's and said to Luke, "I dreamed TCU won." Luke grinned back and said, 'Yeah, in triple overtime. It went to triple overtime.'

"I get goosebumps thinking about it even now," Schreiner said. "I was just so happy for Bram and his mom and his entire family, with his dad passing just a couple of months before. Bram getting that shot and with everything that had taken place, it just seem that was Bram's moment in the spotlight, to show everybody who he is and to write his story.

"He deserved that moment. It all just came full circle. It just made sense. It was just a feel-good story. I never get tired of talking about it."

Neither does Bram's former high school teammate Zach Mafrige, one of those who happily bought a round of Don Julio tequila shots for everyone that night at Morton's.

"We had the MVP trophy on the table next to us," Mafrige said, still amazed more than six years later. "It was quite a night. It was just so hard to believe what we'd just witnessed. It was nothing less than Cloud Nine. I can't think of a better way to go out in your last game."

It was an emotional memory for the man who wasn't

there, too: Trevone Boykin, who watched the game in Dallas, later told Bram he was in tears after the game.

In 2016, speaking to reporters at the 2016 Davy O'Brien Awards dinner in Fort Worth, Boykin said: "Bram did an amazing job in the game. It was so unbelievable to watch, to see the amount of success he's had with everything he's been through. He's a real success story. The whole team's a real success story just from having the courage to keep pushing through."

As for Gary Patterson, by far the most successful head coach in TCU history and recognized as one of the best college football coaches in the country, the Horned Frogs' Alamo Bowl comeback was yet another validation, not just of TCU's program but also of his personal coaching philosophy.

"Nobody here doesn't work hard," Patterson said of the TCU football program from which he would find himself parting ways in November 2021. "That's not a choice. It's what we do. If you want to win championships, that has to be the way it's done. I've been here for going on [20] years. Working hard isn't a choice here. Not for anybody, the head coach, the assistants, the players.

"That's why we have the reputation with the NFL that we do." Patterson says: When TCU players join the NFL, "they don't embarrass the scout who says we should take him. That's the whole story."

• • •

After TCU's astounding comeback, Patterson finally put Bram Kohlhausen on scholarship for his last semester at the school, but the coach is still careful to frame the comeback as a team victory, rather than a single player's individual accomplishment. As good as he was, Patterson notes, it wasn't just about Bram.

"He'll go down in the history of TCU as the engineer of

a great comeback," Patterson said. "We just wanted to play better, make it a ball game and see what happens. Everybody knows the rest of the story.

"I put him on [scholarship] in the spring. He'd worked hard, been a great teammate. We have guys who graduate early and free up scholarships in the spring, and we try to do that for players like Bram."

Especially, perhaps, when that player had just been the architect of TCU's most amazing victory ever and arguably the greatest comeback in college football bowl history.

Bram might have been hinting at that when he visited Patterson in his office not long after that glorious evening in San Antonio.

"Bram came in and said, 'Don't you wish you'd played me more?' " Patterson recalls. "I said, 'Could you beat out Trevone Boykin?' "

The coach, you see, always gets the last word.

Except . . .

Boykin wasn't there on that fateful night at the Alamo Bowl. A no-name backup quarterback looking for redemption in his first and only major college start was.

His name was Bram Kohlhausen.

Epilogue

An Unlikely Hero

A hero is about the shortest-lived profession on earth.
Will Rogers

WHICH BRINGS US BACK full circle to the star of our story, lingering at the fringes of that swarm of dejected Horned Frogs at halftime, staring at a scoreboard that showed TCU down 31-0 to Oregon. Bram Kohlhausen was, at that moment, the most unlikely of heroes, not even expected to be seen on the field again in the second half.

The first half had been a microcosm of Bram's college football career, to that point remarkable only for its unfulfilled promise.

Bram could have easily quit. He could have simply given up, called it a day. Not just Bram, either, but the whole TCU team. But he would not. His teammates would not. Such determination, such perseverance, is the mortar of dreams.

At some point in that eye-rubbing second half, everything coalesced and came together behind Bram's single-minded leadership, his unwillingness to accept defeat. His teammates were inflamed by that spark, and it became a raging purple inferno.

Can lives be changed by a single football game that, in a hundred years, only the record books will remember? Bram Kohlhausen, certainly, will never again be the person he was as he stood there on the Alamodome turf at halftime, disconsolate and disheartened.

Nor, for that matter, will he ever be the same person he was when he and his mother were sharing a victory hug on the Alamo Dome's field. He has grown up since then. Today's Bram Kohlhausen can look back with a critical eye at his own potholed path and see where he veered into the ditch on more than one occasion. And after the Alamo Bowl victory, he admits, he could have handled the sudden notoriety better.

"It impacted me in almost a negative way at first," Bram admits. "I had a huge head afterwards, and nobody could tell me anything. I stopped working out. I rode that euphoria for too long.

"I thought I was 'big man on campus.' I was enjoying people knowing who I was at school. In the short term, I thought it was *my* win. I had a selfish attitude towards what had happened. I know now it was more an accomplishment for the team, the program and the school."

Only a few weeks after that big win in San Antonio, Bram stopped by TCU to say hello to a few old friends, including sports information director Mark Cohen. Kohlhausen was being besieged by requests from the national media, including one of the national network morning talk shows, and Cohen had offered to help him sort out the multitude of demands. Afterward, Cohen offered to give Bram a tour of the Frogs' new facilities at Schollmaier Arena, which had just opened.

"We had just come down on the elevator to the event level," Cohen recalls. "When the doors opened, there was a group of maybe 25 folks, perhaps a few senior alums, also taking a tour. Someone recognized Bram.

"It was like Elvis Presley was in the room," Cohen continues. "They were star-struck. They were posing for pictures with him, asking for autographs. It hit me at that moment: *This guy is a rock star now*."

A few steps away, in TCU's Jane & John Justin Hall of Fame, the two would pause at the display where the Alamo Bowl championship trophy resides. Though Bram has the game's MVP trophy at home, this trophy does not bear his name. It is not his alone.

"I know that trophy sits in the TCU trophy case, symbolizing what we did as a team," Bram says. "Over time, I was able to mature and step back and admire the accomplishment as a team. I like to think I helped propel TCU's program into what it is today. Who knows what recruits were watching that day, how they were impacted by what they saw?"

• • •

What Bram has come to understand, though, is that that kind of fame doesn't go much beyond being an easy conversation starter.

"Realistically," he says, "nobody in the business world really cares."

And when they do care, Bram has discovered, his visibility sometimes has a downside. With fame can come harsher public scrutiny; it's not uncommon for fans to think they have a personal stake in their idol.

During the 2018 U.S. Senate race between Republican incumbent Ted Cruz and Democratic challenger Beto O'Rourke, Bram was in Austin with friends, enjoying a night out on Sixth Street. O'Rourke, the fresh-faced liberal from El Paso, was the talk of the town. Someone handed Bram a T-shirt with Beto's face on it, and Bram pulled it on. He posted a photo of himself wearing the shirt to his Instagram account.

"I honestly wasn't trying to make a political statement," Bram said. "I was just joining in the fun. Everyone was wearing one of those shirts."

Then he began getting pointed messages from "some big TCU donors" who prefer their TCU athletes to be somewhat farther to the right or, at the very least, nonpolitical. Bram didn't want to deal with any controversy and promptly deleted the post. But he says the incident made him more wary about his surroundings, whom he's with, what he's doing and who might be watching or listening.

While Bram sometimes regrets not capitalizing on his Alamo Bowl triumph to give pro football a try — he's had some success as a "walk-on" before, after all — he's focused now on a more long-term future.

His original hope was that it would include sports, although it hasn't turned out that way so far.

After his graduation from TCU, Bram turned his attention to earning an MBA in finance at the University of Houston. He thought he might put his sports background to good use as an NFL sports agent, so in 2021 he forked over $2,000 to the league office to take the NFL test that's required for certification as an agent.

He studied diligently and even took a prep course in Houston before taking the NFL test.

"I thought I did great when I took the test," Bram said. "I even told a buddy that planned on taking it how easy it was and that he'd have no problem with it."

Then he received an e-mail from the NFL office. Needing a 70 to pass, Bram had scored a 68. His disappointment was made even worse by the NFL's policy of offering no feedback to those who don't pass the first time.

"It's just frustrating to have come so close and then not know what questions I missed," Bram said. "I can take it again next year, if I want, but it means coughing up another two grand. The whole experience has kind of turned me off on going in that direction. I'm just not sure it's worth it."

Instead, Bram moved to Austin, to take a position with a venture capital company. He's happy with that decision, he says: "I really enjoy what I'm doing now."

Whether sports figures in Bram's future or not, though, he will always be the hero of the 2016 Alamo Bowl.

No one player wins a football game singlehandedly, but there is no question that TCU could not have won that night without Kohlhausen's inspired leadership and performance under fire. He was at the heart of one of college football's most amazing comebacks.

Bram knows what that win meant to him and his teammates. That second-half comeback salvaged pride, dignity, self-respect. They didn't just come close; they didn't just score a "moral victory" by making a game of it. They finished the job.

"It'll be with me forever," Bram says. "People seem to always remember that game. To this day, I'll go into a business meeting, or I'll be at a party and friends will introduce me as the guy who won that game against Oregon. It's a great icebreaker. Anyone watching college football remembers that game."

Not long ago, Bram was at Houston's Royal Oaks Golf Club for a game with a couple of friends, both of them players with the NFL. He was about to tee off when the cart boy asked him if he was *the* Bram Kohlhausen, the one who had led TCU to victory in that famed Alamo Bowl game.

Answered in the affirmative, the cart boy proffered a pen and paper: Could he get Bram's autograph?

Bram obliged, but not without some embarrassment, signing his name and returning the pen to the youth.

"You know," he told the cart boy, nodding at his NFL friends, "these are the guys you should be getting autographs from."

The kid shrugged and almost reluctantly handed Bram's friends the pen.

The cart boy didn't know those NFL guys, but he knew the name of Bram Kohlhausen.

For him, as for thousands of fans who shared the fantastical roller-coaster ride that was the 2016 Alamo Bowl — whether in the stands of the Alamodome, watching it unfold on TV or hearing the legend of the game recalled later — it is a name unlikely to be forgotten.

For anyone who follows TCU football, it is a name that conjures pure magic — purple magic.

Where They Are Now

KEEPING IN MIND that the coaching carousel can spin rapidly, here's a look at where several of the players in this story found themselves as this book went to press in early 2022.

Donna Kohlhausen still lives in Houston, still golfs frequently and teaches law classes at the University of Houston.

Dash Kohlhausen just passed his 10-year anniversary as a corporate attorney with Landry's Restaurants. His office is in Houston.

Gareth Kohlhausen works in real estate at Latipac Commercial in Houston.

Gary Patterson and TCU parted ways eight games into the 2021 season. The Horned Frogs were 3-5 overall and 1-4 in Big 12 play at the time. Patterson declined an opportunity to finish the season, and veteran assistant Jerry Kill took over briefly as interim head coach before TCU brought in Sonny Dykes from SMU as its new head football coach. Patterson was in his 21st season at the TCU helm and is the winningest head coach in the school's history.

Doug Meacham left TCU to become offensive coordinator for the Kansas Jayhawks in 2017 but lasted just a season and a half. He was hired as offensive coordinator for the XFL's St. Louis franchise, but he had already returned to TCU as inside wide receivers coach before the XFL filed for bankruptcy during the coronavirus pandemic. He was a casualty of the purge when Sonny Dykes replaced Patterson.

Sonny Cumbie was Texas Tech offensive coordinator and quarterbacks coach when the 2021 season began and became interim head coach when Matt Wells was fired in late October. New Red Raiders head coach Jerry McGuire announced that he will retain Cumbie as his offensive coordinator and QB coach for 2022.

Mack Brown, whose incisive commentary in the TV booth made him look like a modern-day football Nostradamus during the Alamo Bowl, stepped out of the booth to become head coach at the University of North Carolina. His Tar Heels, ranked No. 10 in 2021 preseason polls, stumbled to a 6-5 record, including a stunning 34-30 loss to North Carolina State in its final regular season game when the Wolfpack rallied from 9 points down with less than two minutes to play.

Kliff Kingsbury, who helped recruit Bram to Houston, went on to a successful run as head coach at Texas Tech and is now the head coach of the NFL's Arizona Cardinals.

Kevin Sumlin, briefly a Kohlhausen family neighbor in Houston, compiled a 51-26 record over six seasons at Texas A&M after leaving UH but had only one winning season in the SEC. He was fired after the 2017 season. He became head coach at the University of Arizona in 2018 and went 9-20 in three seasons. He was fired on Dec. 12, 2020, the day after the Wildcats suffered their worst loss ever to in-state rival Arizona State, 70-7.

Reuben Ale, who was Bram's head coach at Los Angeles Harbor College, died in 2020 at age 55 after a 24-year coaching career.

Dick Lowe, the legendary Fort Worth oilman noted for

his support of TCU football, died in 2020 at age 92.

Trevone Boykin, the most tragic figure in any story about that unforgettable night, ended up watching the game at home in Dallas while playing dominoes with his mom.

After the River Walk incident, Boykin pleaded no contest to a count of resisting arrest and received a year's deferred adjudication probation in June of 2016.

After signing with the Seattle Seahawks and playing five games backing up Russell Wilson there in 2016, he was arrested in Dallas on charges of public intoxication and misdemeanor marijuana possession on March 17, 2017, after a car in which he was a passenger struck a tavern, hitting several people on the sidewalk.

Most disturbing were the allegations of domestic violence. His girlfriend, Shabrika Bailey, reported that Boykin broke her jaw on both sides in March 2018, rendering her unconscious and requiring a hospital stay to have her jaw wired shut. The Seahawks cut Boykin in the wake of the allegation after he'd spent 2017 on their practice squad, and he subsequently was charged in Texas with additional misdemeanors.

In February 2020, Boykin received a three-year prison sentence after pleading guilty to aggravated assault and witness tampering in the 2018 beating. He was also sentenced to 180 days in Tarrant County Jail for misdemeanor theft charges. Boykin was incarcerated in the Byrd Unit in Huntsville. His projected release date is Oct. 31, 2022.

About the Author

JIM "REVO" REEVES, an award-winning sports reporter and columnist at the *Fort Worth Star-Telegram* over four decades, has covered 29 World Series, a dozen Super Bowls and numerous NBA championships and Stanley Cup Finals. In 1987 he was nominated for a Pulitzer Prize for his coverage of the sale of the Texas Rangers to a group headed by George W. Bush.

He was named Texas Sports Columnist of the Year on multiple occasions by both the Associated Press Managing Editors Association and the Associated Press Sports Editors Association. The only sportswriter ever honored with the national Schieffer School of Journalism Ethics Award from TCU, in 2007, he has been a four-time finalist for the Baseball Writers' Association of America Career Excellence Award.

Reeves is the author of *Dallas Cowboys: The Legends of America's Team* (Great Texas Line Press). After retiring from daily journalism, he wrote a column for ESPN.com and now completes assignments for the *Texas Rangers Yearbook* and other publications. He and his wife, Karen, live in Dalworthington Gardens, Texas.